MALCOLM HILLIER'S
WREATHS AND GARLANDS

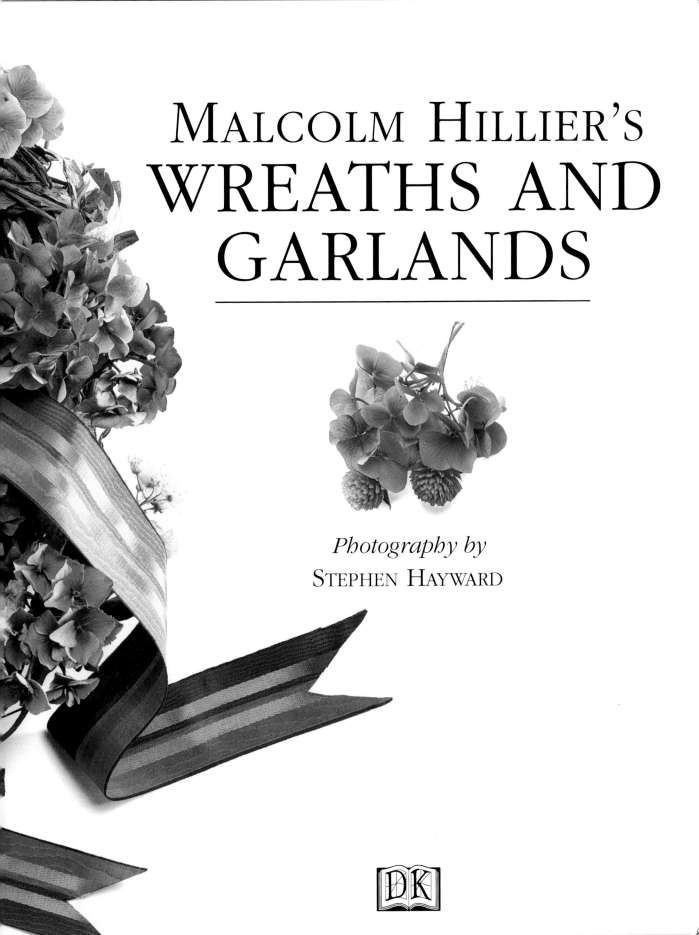

MALCOLM HILLIER'S
WREATHS AND
GARLANDS

Photography by
STEPHEN HAYWARD

A DK PUBLISHING BOOK

Project Editor	Gillian Roberts
Art Editor	Deborah Myatt
Managing Editor	Mary-Clare Jerram
Managing Art Editor	Spencer Holbrook
Production	Adrian Gathercole
US Editors	Julee Binder
	Ray Rogers

First American Edition, 1994
4 6 8 10 9 7 5

Published in the United States by DK Publishing, Inc.
95 Madison Avenue, New York, NY 10016

Copyright © 1994 Dorling Kindersley Limited, London
Text copyright © 1994 Malcolm Hillier

Visit us on the World Wide Web at
http://www.dk.com

Library of Congress Cataloging-in-Publication Data

Hillier, Malcolm.
Wreaths and garlands / by Malcolm Hillier. -- 1st American ed.
p.   cm.
Includes index.
ISBN 1-56458-618-9
1. Wreaths   I. Title
TT899.75.H54   1994
745.92--dc20   94-6292
CIP

Computer page makeup by Mark Bracey and Deborah Myatt,
Dorling Kindersley, Great Britain

Text film output by The Right Type, Great Britain

Reproduced by Colourscan, Singapore

Printed and bound in Italy by Graphicom

CONTENTS

FOREWORD

MY INTRODUCTION TO THE MAGIC OF GARLANDS was when, as children, we would make daisy chains. On those long days of summer, the lawn always seemed to be well supplied with daisies, despite my father's arduous hand-weeding sessions, and I have always had an affection for these beautiful but little-considered flowers.

For this book, I've drawn together a great range of ingredients – sometimes plain ordinary, sometimes exotic, but always as lovely as all plants are – to create colorful and exciting arrangements to garland and swag, to hang and drape, to swirl and entwine. There are fresh and dried flower pictures for the wall, and all manner of garlands to dress staircases, windows, fireplaces, and columns for grand celebrations and special festivities. There are simple spice and herb wreaths and other everyday decorations to hang in the kitchen, sitting room, or bedroom that will give endless pleasure not only to you, their maker, but to everyone who sees them.

You need not be an expert to enjoy a few hours' garlanding, for there's a full description of how to make everything in the book. Better still, substitute ingredients of your own choosing for those of mine, and make something that is yours in a very special way.

Malcolm Hillier

PRACTICAL
ESSENTIALS

Tools and Materials
Plant Ingredients
Step-by-step Techniques

TOOLS AND MATERIALS

BEFORE YOU START making your own wreaths, garlands, and other hanging decorations, it's handy to know what tools and materials you need to have by you. Of the essential few, a really good-quality pair of florist's scissors is the most important – preferably scissors that can cut wires as well as woody plant stems.

A knife with a short, sharp-edged blade that is not too flexible; a variety of fine, medium, and heavy-gauge floral wires in 12in (30cm) lengths; and a spool or two of fine wire are other essentials. A glue gun is also a useful item, making quick work of many jobs that could once have been done only by wiring.

◄ **WET FOAM WREATH BASE**
Excellent for use with fresh flowers, these are sold in a variety of shapes and several different sizes.

DRY FOAM BALLS ▼
Use these just as they are to make hanging dried flower spheres.

THICK TWINE ▼
With its rough, slightly hairy texture, twine is ideal for non-slip ties; use also as a base for lightweight garlands.

WET FOAM BRICK ▲
These can be cut to fit into any lined container that you choose for an arrangement of fresh flowers and foliage.

STURDY CORD ▼
All but the chunkiest of flexible garlands can be wired onto sturdy cord.

TWISTED STEM CIRCLE ▼
Bases that are formed from natural plant materials suit both fresh and dried flowers: for speed and ease, you can buy them ready-made.

RUSH HALF-BASKET WITH TWIG HANDLE ▼
Hang lush, flamboyant decorations (dried or fresh) up on a wall in a basket that has one flat side.

RAFFIA STRANDS ▼
You'll find numerous uses for raffia, from braided wreath bases to single-strand ties.

◄ CHICKEN WIRE
Moss-filled chicken wire is the base of many arrangements: use 1in (2.5cm) gauge mesh.

FLORAL TAPE ▲
This binding tape is useful for covering wired flower stems.

A VARIETY OF RIBBONS ►
To adorn any arrangement: wire-edged ribbon holds its shape; paper ribbon curls well; woven ribbon is fine for binding; coiled paper ribbon fans out into bows.

2¾in (7cm) wire-edged ribbon

WIRE CUTTERS ▲
Not essential, but handy for cutting thicker-gauge wires.

1in (2.5cm) wire-edged ribbon

BUN MOSS ▲
The cushiony mounds dry particularly well, and retain their color and soft texture.

SPHAGNUM MOSS ▲
Use this kind of moss as the filling for chicken-wire bases.

FLORIST'S SCISSORS ▲
A good pair will be more than worth the investment.

2in (5cm) wire-edged ribbon

REINDEER MOSS ▲
Its neutral color makes this a fine background material.

SPANISH MOSS ▲
This versatile moss comes dyed *(left)* or natural *(right)*.

PRUNERS ▲
This cutting tool deals well with thick or tough stems.

⅜in (1cm) paper ribbon

SHARP KNIFE ▲
Where fresh flower stems need scraping, use a knife.

GLUE GUN AND GLUE STICKS ▼
Look for a low-melt gun: it's the safest and easiest to use.

SPOOL WIRE ▼
Use spool wire for all but the very finest wiring jobs.

heavy-gauge floral wires

medium-gauge floral wires

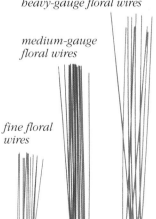

1½in (4cm) woven ribbon

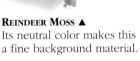

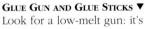

FINE SPOOL WIRE ▲
Ideal for fine wiring work.

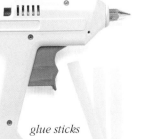

glue sticks

fine floral wires

FLORAL WIRES ►
For wiring single heads and bunches: in several gauges.

fanned, coiled paper ribbon

FRESH FLOWERS

ROSES, FREESIAS, DAFFODILS, carnations, and the ubiquitous chrysanthemum: look for them at your nearest florist's shop even in the depths of a severe winter, and you're almost sure to find them in abundant supply. These as well as numerous other varieties are nowadays so readily available that making up fresh flower garlands for special celebrations has become an activity that's possible at any time of year.

Yet I'd still rather use flowers that have been grown in their own natural season. From the austere simplicity of winter, the freshness of springtime, the exuberance of high summer, to the glowing embers of autumn: each one of the seasons has a definite mood, which is reflected in the flowers that are about at that time. Acquaint yourself with all the different kinds to discover which you like using best.

Guernsey lily
The flowers of this nerine variety bloom in autumn and have graceful wavy-edged petals

Tuberose
This summer-flowering Mexican plant has an extremely pervasive perfume

Chrysanthemum
Spray chrysanthemums, which carry several small flowers on each stem, are more suitable for garland- and wreath-making than large single blooms

Dendrobium orchid
Exotic and intensely colored, orchids are surprisingly robust

Freesia
These look delicate but are an excellent choice for arrangements that have to last for several days or longer

Tulip
The double flowers of 'Angélique' fill the air with their sweet scent

PREPARING FRESH FLOWERS

WHETHER YOU CUT flowers from your garden or buy them from a florist's shop or market, it's always sensible to prepare them before you start to make up any arrangement. Flowers that look strong and healthy have a head start on limp, tired blooms, so pick stems that are in the very best condition. Of the more usual kinds, roses, carnations, alstroemeria, and pinks last well. Sweet peas, though wonderfully scented, fade in a day.

To condition flowers ready to use, fill a bucket or some other roomy container with warm water. Take a sharp-bladed knife, and cut the stems at an angle. Strip off lower leaves and scrape 1½in (4cm) at the ends of the stems. Place the flowers in the water, then leave them there for two hours or so. Split any stems that are woody, such as those of lilac, after the cutting and scraping treatment.

Rose
Choose miniature or spray roses for small designs

Golden wattle
This species of the native Australian acacia was once used for fencing, hence its name

Carnation
The scarlet-striped petals of the carnation 'Master Stuart' *make a strikingly strong statement; shown below them, sprays have less showy flowers that last just as well*

Delphinium
Purists may well insist on blue for this classic cottage-garden plant, but do look for hybrid forms in whites, pinks, lilacs, and rich purples: they're also very beautiful

Anemone
Anemone coronaria *De Caen Series has large flat flowers of red, white, blue, or white flushed red, as here*

FRESH FOLIAGE

IF FLOWERS ARE most often the brilliant stars in fresh arrangements, foliage forms the perfect unifying backdrop for their colorful display. Fresh foliage is there for you to choose in so broad a variety that you need never be short of the exact right thing for whatever hanging decoration you're wanting to make. Nor is it necessarily green: many species are specially grown for their attractively variegated leaves.

For cut flower decorations in vases, I always like to use the flowers' own foliage; but with garlands, it may be a different matter. Leaves of some flowers, for example carnations and roses, either are unsuitably shaped for filling in, or don't last well. So when planning your decorations, select foliage that is in harmony with them, whether it's strands of smilax for a garland or tufts of spruce for a bold swag.

Eucalyptus
Rounded, as here, or long and slender, eucalyptus leaves have a pungent, aromatic scent

Dogwood
The finely cream-edged leaves of Cornus alba *'Elegantissima' – a kind of redtwig dogwood – are borne on slender, graceful stems*

Viburnum
Late-winter flowering evergreens, such as Viburnum tinus *(also called laurustinus), are doubly useful*

Blue spruce
Agreeably chunky, the silver-blue branches of this conifer will last for two weeks or so out of water: such foliage is perfect for carefree, long-holiday decorations

Hebe
Splashes of creamy white brighten the evergreen leaves of this compact, bushy shrub

PREPARING FRESH FOLIAGE

ALL FRESH FOLIAGE needs some preparation if it's to last. Run some warm water into a bucket or other roomy container: a small amount will do. Cut the stems across at an angle, using a sharp knife, and scrape 1½in (4cm) at the bottom of each one. For hard, woody stems only, split the ends. Leave the foliage in the water for at least two hours; if your schedule allows, overnight is even better. Foliage that starts to look tired can be revived by putting already prepared stems into very hot water. After five minutes, top up the hot with cold water and allow the foliage to condition as described above.

Smilax
This climber will almost twine itself through garlands

Bells of Ireland
The leaves of this plant are of less interest than the large green calyx that surrounds each flower

Fishtail palm
Unusual leaves add a touch of drama to fresh arrangements of uncomplicated plant materials

Cypress
Sprays of compact and spreading foliage make a good background for flat wall hangings

Rosemary
Hang herbal wreaths where they can waft their scent: aromatic foliage readily yields up its perfume when brushed against or crushed

Tree ivy
This vigorous ivy has large, glossy evergreen leaves; its white summer flowers give way to black fruits

Tree asparagus
Frothy tufts suit any delicate design

DRIED PLANT MATERIAL

IT MAKES EXCELLENT SENSE to use dried flowers and foliage, seedheads, and pods in many of your garlands, swags, and hanging creations. Arrangements that have taken hours of work to put together will never flag or expire, and you can make them whenever you like from materials that are always available. But don't keep them for more than nine months or so: after this time they begin to look a trifle sad.

Flower markets, garden centers, and florists, and even some stores specializing in interior design and housewares, are all worth a look into for the tantalizing selection of dried and preserved plant material that's nowadays for sale. Cultivating plants yourself, either in the garden or in containers, then drying them, is a satisfying way of obtaining those particular ingredients that you want to use most often.

Miniature globe thistle
Spiky leaves set off these steel blue heads

Artemisia
This tall plant is grown for its willowy silver-gray foliage

Larkspur
Cultivated plants can be blue, white, or pink, but their wild cousins are usually violet

Sunflower
Dried blooms keep all the brilliance of fresh flowers: the crumpled petals swiftly perk up in a cloud of steam

Cluster-flowered everlasting
Like all everlastings, this variety is superb for drying

Field poppy
With their crisp, strong form, poppy seedheads work best in designs of bold materials

STEAMING FLOWERS

Revive dried flowers that are squashed by holding them in the steam of a boiling kettle. Their petals will start to flop in moments. Holding the flower away from the steam and upside down, blow up quite gently into the petals: the shape is soon set.

after: revived

before: squashed

Strelitzia •
Palmlike bird of paradise leaves dry into wonderfully twisted and sinuous shapes

Lavender
If you're growing this scented favorite to dry yourself, pick stems as the flowers begin to open for the best results •

Rose
Rosa 'Golden Time', a modern hybrid tea rose, bears its compact, open flowers on abundantly leafy stems •

Yarrow
Any arrangement of dried plant materials is certain to make a major statement if it includes these large flat heads of golden flowers •

Statice
These fanned clusters of very small flowers come in numerous shades of blue, red, white, yellow, and purple •

Copper beech
Preserving in glycerin will keep foliage pliant; this had a bit of purple dye added to enhance its natural coloring of bronze-red

Horsetail
Also known as Dutch rush, these decorative dried stems are from a plant best kept out of the garden: it's a rampant weed

Cockscomb celosia
The rich reds, yellows, oranges, and purples of these velvety crests glint with a lustrous silver sheen

Prince's feather
Tall and bushy, the flower spires of this amaranthus species may be colored burgundy red, as here, or pink or green

Bottlebrush
The scarlet clusters that surround these stems are the showy slender stamens of tiny flowers

PRESERVING FLOWERS AND FOLIAGE

PRESERVING FLOWERS and foliage yourself is not at all difficult. Many well-known flower species can simply be hung up, heads down, to dry in a cool and dark place. Strawflowers, statice, hybrid tea roses, and larkspur can all be dried in this way, and last well. Be sure there's no hint of moisture, or the flowers will mold before they've completely dried out. Encase flowers like peonies, lilies, and lovely old-fashioned roses in silica gel crystals to achieve the best results.

As for foliage: that of beech, oak, and ivy responds particularly well to being preserved in glycerin. Add a dash of dye in an appropriate shade, if you want, to provide the foliage with lasting color of a good density. If you become really interested in the drying of plant materials, consult one of the many books available. My *Complete Book of Dried Flowers* gives the techniques in detail, and design guidelines too.

Shepherd's purse
The branching stems of Lunaria minima are covered in a mass of beautiful lime green rustling seedheads

Rose
The subtle creamy-pink shades of Rosa 'Europa' become even softer when the blooms dry

Love-in-a-mist
Dried just as the flower petals fall, these seedheads are at their plum-green best

Strawflower
Aglow with vibrant color, strawflowers make a magnificent garden display and dry superbly well

Tree ivy
Given the glycerin and dye treatment, this useful evergreen retains all the vigor of fresh foliage

Sunray
Dainty Helipterum roseum dries just as easily as the related strawflower

FRUITS AND VEGETABLES

A SHORT, UNHURRIED STROLL through a farmer's market will furnish you with a whole host of wonderful new ideas for wreath and garland ingredients. So often, we shop for vegetables and fruits thinking of them only as food that we tend to forget just how beautiful are their natural forms and colors. Even a leaf of the humble cabbage creates a marvelous effect.

Consider vicious red chilies, dark purple exotic mangosteens, cloves of garlic flushed pink through their tight papery skins, sticks of woodsy cinnamon bark, the sculpture of tropical pods. Possibilities soon appear if you let your imagination wander a little.

String of garlic
The compact heads are a superb shape but do carry a perfume that's not to everyone's taste

Physalis
This member of the tomato family is also called Cape gooseberry: pull back the petal-like calyx to reveal the juicy orange fruits

Bird's eye chilies
You can thread these together for Christmas tree garlands, or wire them into wreaths for a kitchen or pantry

Cinnamon bark
Ribbon-tied bundles are a fragrant addition to herb and spice wreaths

Pink pepperberries
Not genuine peppercorns, but still an edible seasoning, these decorative trusses are the fruit of the shrub, Schinus molle

Baby globe artichoke
These specially cultivated, miniature editions of the full-sized vegetables are best used fresh

Savoy cabbage
Add a dramatic touch to an otherwise plain design with a leaf of deep-etched veins and crinkles

Walnuts in shell
Hard-shelled nuts can
be burnished with gold
or silver spray paint

Tropical seedpods
Groups of these fascinating
objects make decorations of
spectacular simplicity

Pattypan squash
Use bite-sized vegetables
for small-scale designs

Whiteheart cherry
Fruits in pairs are easy
to hook into garlands

Tamarillo
Ruby red fruits are a
must for festive swags

Pine cones
These can look rustic or grand,
depending on how you use them

Dried mushroom cone
The edges are thin and
brittle: handle with care

Hop vines
Hang garlands made with these
trails away from the hurly-burly
of a crowd, or they will become
crushed and disintegrate

Crabapples
Unblemished fruits on
the stem last a couple
of weeks out of water

Pomegranate
Heavy fruits like these
should be hollowed out
before being wired into
an arrangement

Mangosteen
The thick, fibrous skin
of this Malaysian fruit
encloses juicy segments
of sweet-acid flesh

Lime
One vibrant color enlivens
a design where subdued
tints predominate

Red chilies
No matter that these wrinkle
as they dry: their shiny
redness blazes on

Clementines
The attractiveness of citrus
fruits is doubled when the
leaves are still attached

21

WIRING PLANT MATERIAL

OFTEN, YOU CAN MAKE UP wreaths, swags, and hanging arrangements using fresh and dried flowers and leaves on their own stems. With some designs, however, you will want to be able to get a single flower or bunch to lie or point just so, in one particular direction, and this is where wiring plant material comes in. Although most wiring techniques are not at all hard to do, some can be a little bit tricky.

If you have a substantial amount of wiring to do, such as when making up several lengths of garlanding, leave yourself lots of time – it isn't a quick job. Four of the sequences here illustrate easy techniques that you can use to attach either individual pieces or bunches of plant material into a wreath or garland base. Where a visibly neat, tidy finish is important, complete your wired work using floral tape.

WIRING A SHORT, FRAGILE, OR WOODY STEM

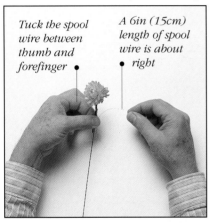

Tuck the spool wire between thumb and forefinger •

A 6in (15cm) length of spool wire is about • *right*

Rotate the stem and floral wire between your thumb and forefinger •

Keep a taut hold of the spool wire •

Finish a little way beyond the end of • *the stem*

1 Hold the stem and a floral wire together. Put a piece of spool wire next to them.

2 Twist the spool wire, from its midpoint, up the stem. Wind it over itself at the top.

3 Continue to twist the wire down over itself, the floral wire, and length of the stem.

WIRING A BUNCH OF DRIED OR FRESH PLANT MATERIAL

Select a 14in (35cm) floral wire that's strong enough to support the bunch •

Spiraling the wire over itself holds • *it securely*

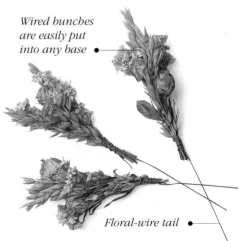

Wired bunches are easily put into any base •

Floral-wire tail •

1 Place a floral wire against the stems and extending above the head of the bunch.

2 Bend the long end of the floral wire across the front of the bunch, then around it.

3 Twist the wire over itself down to the ends of the stems, leaving a longish tail.

WIRING A SOFT STEM

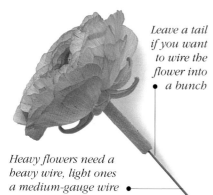

Leave a tail if you want to wire the flower into a bunch

Heavy flowers need a heavy wire, light ones a medium-gauge wire

1 Push a piece of floral wire up through the middle of the stem and into the flower.

WIRING EITHER A HOLLOW OR A SOFT STEM

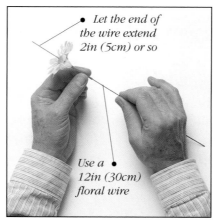

Let the end of the wire extend 2in (5cm) or so

Use a 12in (30cm) floral wire

1 Push a piece of floral wire up through the stem, then on beyond the flower head.

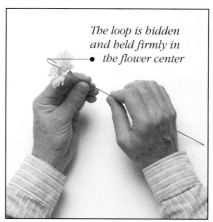

The loop is hidden and held firmly in the flower center

2 Bend a loop in the end of the floral wire and pull it back into the flower center.

USING FLORAL TAPE

FOR SOME VERY SPECIAL arrangements, you may want to get a finish that withstands close scrutiny. Bridal headdresses, for example, are seen from all sides and angles, even from underneath. With designs of this sort, it's best to hide the rather unsightly stems of wired flowers and leaves. You can do this by covering them over with floral tape. This is available in pale or dark green or brown for color-matching to the flower stem and looks quite natural.

Bridal headdress, top view

Underneath of bridal headdress

Floral tape covers over the flower stems and the wire that binds them to the floral-wire base of this bridal headdress

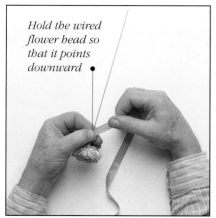

Hold the wired flower head so that it points downward

1 Lay a long piece of floral tape, at an angle, close to the base of the wired flower.

Keep tension on the tape with your free hand as you twirl the stem

2 Twirl the flower stem with one hand so that the tape spirals tightly down the stem.

FLEXIBLE BASE TECHNIQUES

IF THE GARLAND you are wanting to make is to frame a window or doorway, hang in swags against a wall or table front, or spiral around a column or pole, it is best to put it together on a flexible base such as wire, thick twine, light cord, or soft rope. All are excellent for dainty, lightweight garlands of fresh flowers.

The basic technique for making garlands of this kind is simple. Before you start on one of these projects, though, bear in mind that it takes time to create a very long garland. Set aside several hours if you want to do it in one go. Garlands of heavy plant material are best made on a rigid base *(see page 26)*.

MAKING A GARLAND ON A THICK TWINE BASE

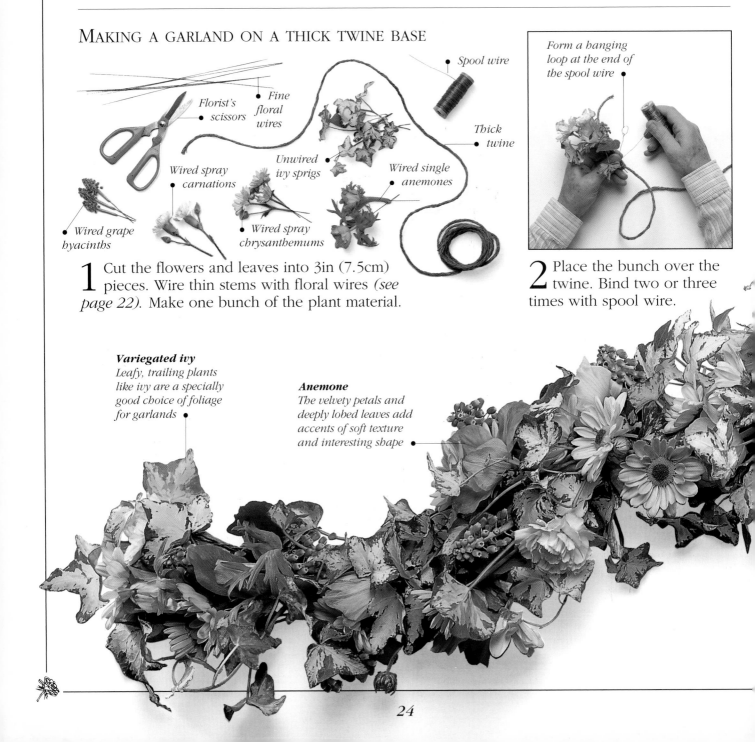

Spool wire

Florist's scissors

Fine floral wires

Thick twine

Wired spray carnations

Unwired ivy sprigs

Wired single anemones

Wired grape hyacinths

Wired spray chrysanthemums

Form a hanging loop at the end of the spool wire

1 Cut the flowers and leaves into 3in (7.5cm) pieces. Wire thin stems with floral wires *(see page 22)*. Make one bunch of the plant material.

2 Place the bunch over the twine. Bind two or three times with spool wire.

Variegated ivy
Leafy, trailing plants like ivy are a specially good choice of foliage for garlands

Anemone
The velvety petals and deeply lobed leaves add accents of soft texture and interesting shape

A firm turn of the wire around the back of the bunch holds it in place

Add bunch after bunch to finish the garland

3 Pass the spool back up between the bunch and the twine. Pull it down on the other side, preventing the wire from unraveling.

4 Make another bunch of the plant material. Put it over the first bunch so that its head overlaps the stems of the previous bunch.

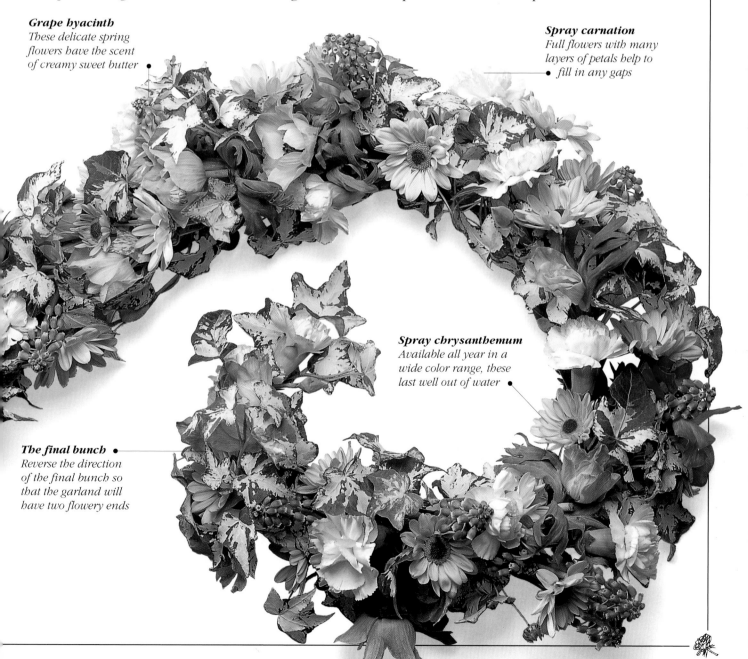

Grape hyacinth
These delicate spring flowers have the scent of creamy sweet butter

Spray carnation
Full flowers with many layers of petals help to fill in any gaps

Spray chrysanthemum
Available all year in a wide color range, these last well out of water

The final bunch
Reverse the direction of the final bunch so that the garland will have two flowery ends

RIGID BASE TECHNIQUES

ALL WREATHS are best made up on some kind of a rigid base that will easily support all the flowers, foliage, fruits, seedheads, and other plant material that you want to place into it. The most useful and versatile base is a tube made of chicken wire rolled around a solid stuffing of dry sphagnum moss. Use this for making heavy garlands and swags also. Just leave the two tube ends unjoined, and then bend the tube to the shape that you require.

A copper-wire frame clad with moss can be used for a lightweight wreath. If you want a base that is quick to do and looks lovely in its own right, a braided raffia ring might be your choice. All these bases are suitable for use with dried ingredients. Wreaths of fresh flowers need a wet foam base *(see page 74),* especially if they contain short-lived flowers. Designs that call for solid shapes are easy to make on a mattress base *(see pages 30–31).*

MAKING A CIRCULAR CHICKEN WIRE AND MOSS BASE

Snip the chicken wire to the size you need with wire cutters

Spool wire

Florist's scissors

Dry sphagnum moss

Wire cutters

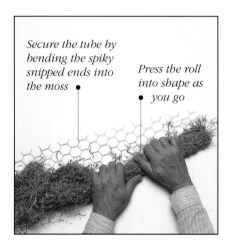

Secure the tube by bending the spiky snipped ends into the moss

Press the roll into shape as you go

1 Slightly flatten the chicken wire and lay it on a firm surface. Put the moss along one long side, distributing it evenly.

2 Starting from one end, roll the chicken wire with the moss to get a thin, firm tube.

Hold the tube steady with one hand

Bend the tube with your other hand

Have the cut side of the chicken wire on the inner edge of the ring

Use the free end of wire to lace the two tube ends together

3 Grasp the tube with both hands and, again working from one end, bend it around so that the two ends butt together to form a ring.

4 To join up the ring, run spool wire back and forth from one end of the tube to the other. Cut the wire and neatly tie off its ends.

COVERING A STORE-BOUGHT WIRE FRAME WITH MOSS

Spool wire

Florist's scissors

Double-ring copper-wire frame

Dry sphagnum moss

To finish, tie off the spool wire to the first knot, and tuck the two ends into the moss

1 Separate the moss into big handfuls. Tie the free end of spool wire to the outer ring of the frame in a firm knot.

2 Using spool wire, bind the moss handfuls to the frame to cover it completely.

MAKING A BRAIDED RAFFIA RING

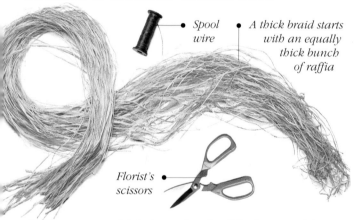

Spool wire

A thick braid starts with an equally thick bunch of raffia

Florist's scissors

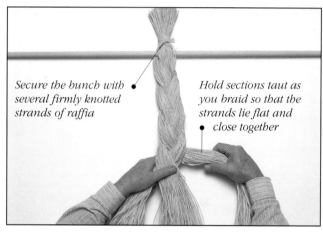

Secure the bunch with several firmly knotted strands of raffia

Hold sections taut as you braid so that the strands lie flat and close together

1 Prepare a thick bunch of raffia by combing through the length with your fingers. This separates the strands and untangles any knots.

2 Bind one end of the bunch and tie it to a firm support. Divide into three. Braid left and right alternately over the center section.

Tidy up the braid by cutting off any short strands of raffia that stick out

Leave straggly ends on the loop, or cut them off if you prefer a neater finish

3 Holding on to the free end, untie the braid from its support. Cross over the two ends, forming a ring. Bind the join with spool wire.

4 Make a thin raffia braid for a hanging loop. Tie it over the join, and cross its two ends into a bow. Bind with a single strand of raffia.

COVERING A CHICKEN WIRE AND MOSS BASE

6in (15cm) medium-gauge floral wires

Handmade chicken wire and dry moss wreath base

Spanish moss, dyed green

14in (35cm) heavy-gauge floral wire

Florist's scissors

Drape the moss over the ring to cover both edges

Floral-wire hairpins

1 Make the base *(see page 26)*. Separate the Spanish moss into thick strands. Bend the medium floral wires in half to form hairpins.

2 Attach the moss: push the hairpins through the base, then bend their ends back in.

Keep the ends 1in (2.5cm) apart as you push them through

Wire loop for hanging

Give the wire end a final firm tug away from the base before bending it back

Bend up the wire loop to hang the wreath

3 Loop the center of the heavy-gauge floral wire. Push both of its ends from the back of the base, at top midcenter, to the front.

4 Holding onto the looped wire center, bend one of the ends, then push it back into the base. Secure the second end in the same way.

Wreath base, covered with Spanish moss

Wired bunches of dried flowers and preserved leaves

Florist's scissors

Wired single pine cones

Unwired single dried peony heads, refreshed in steam

Push the wire through and back into the base

5 Refresh dried flowers (optional, *see page 17)*. Wire single cones, and bunches of the dried flowers and foliage *(see page 22)*.

6 Arrange the background (here, cones) in a pattern that is balanced yet informal.

All the bunches should face the same way •

Flowers with strong stalks are simply pushed in: no need to • *wire them*

7 Push in the next layer (here, preserved ivy, with dried strawflowers and roses in wired bunches). Keep the colors evenly distributed.

8 Add the last layer (here, single large heads of dried peonies). Using two shades of the same color gives the design an extra interest.

Peony
Dried flowers often have squashed petals but will blossom again if bathed in a cloud of steam •

Pine cone
Wire cones without stalks by twisting a floral wire around the scales at the base •

Ivy
Preserved in a solution of glycerin and green dye, these have all the suppleness and glossy color of fresh leaves

Rose
Store deep-colored dried flowers in a nest of acid-free tissue paper •

Strawflower
Growing these is little bother, and they dry beautifully •

MAKING A CHICKEN WIRE AND MOSS MATTRESS BASE

- *Wire cutters*
- *Floral-wire hairpins*
- *Florist's scissors*
- *Chicken wire*
- *Sphagnum moss*
- *Piece of tree bark*

1 Use the moss dry for a dried arrangement, damp for a fresh one. Place it on one half of the chicken wire, in about the right shape.

First corner, bent into a curve *Press the spiky wire edges into the moss*

2 Fold over the other half of chicken wire. Bend in the four corners to create a circle.

Pin across the wire mesh, not through the holes

3 For a large mattress, push in a number of floral-wire hairpins to hold the moss firmly in place. Space them apart at regular intervals.

Secure the bark (or other object) in at least two places

4 To attach a piece of bark (or other object), thread a medium-gauge floral wire through the wire base. Tie it tightly around the object.

ATTACHING THE DECORATIVE PLANT MATERIAL

- *Fine floral wires*
- *Unwired crabapples*
- *Florist's scissors*
- *Finished base, front view*
- *Medium-gauge floral wires*
- *Wired chestnuts*
- *Wired cypress foliage*

1 Wire the crabapples, using the fruits singly and in groups, and bunches of foliage (*see page 22*). Stick a floral wire into each chestnut.

Central bunches stick up *Fan out side bunches*

2 Push the foliage into the base. Overlap each layer so that the stems are hidden.

For a secure attachment, poke in the wire at an oblique angle

Mix the fruits in bunches, pairs, and singly

3 Wire in the nuts, pushing the floral wire of each all the way through the mattress base. Bend the wire back into the moss to anchor it.

4 Attach the crabapples, pushing their floral wires through and back into the base. Add more fruits and nuts to get a balanced effect.

Chestnut
Put a dot of strong glue on the end of the floral wire, if necessary, to keep it in place

Cypress
Choose plant ingredients that will work with you to achieve the look you're after: the soft, flattened sprays of aromatic cypress foliage fall in place almost by themselves

Crabapple
Groups and single fruits create a pleasing pattern that looks spontaneous yet well balanced

Filling the gaps
When the arrangement appears finished, prop it upright and stand back: holes and gaps that you may not have seen close up are usually revealed from a distance

Bark
A single ingredient of interest may be the starting point for a whole arrangement: my tree idea came from this mossy piece of bark

DESIGNS
FOR EVERY
OCCASION

Wreaths, Rings, Circlets
Garlands, Swags, Festoons
Hanging Plant Pictures

AROMATIC HERB WREATH

THE KITCHEN IS THE PERFECT PLACE to hang this colorful wreath of dried country herbs and spices. Choose a door or wall near your food preparation area, but away from steam and moisture, where you can enjoy its sweetly aromatic perfume while you are working. If you decide to use very bright flowers, like the orange marigolds that I've included, find a position where the wreath can hang out of direct light: bright sunlight, especially, will bleach its colors. Mix your selection of seedheads and flowering herbs to get a good variety of colors, shapes, and textures. A nicely personal touch would be to use herbs that you've grown yourself. Most dry well, although leafy types do tend to turn brown.

Salvia horminum
This color is part of the Art Shades Series: *the dusky purple-blue stays true even when the plant is dried*

Pink pepperberries
Slightly piquant in taste, these berries come from a small shrub native to South America

WHAT YOU WILL NEED

- *14in (35cm) diameter ready-made twisted stem circle*
- *Glue gun (optional)*
- *Few natural raffia strands*
- *Medium-gauge floral wires*
- *60 field poppy seedheads*
- *20 marigolds*
- *4 stalks pink pepperberries*
- *25 stems blue* Salvia horminum
- *50 stems sweet marjoram*
- *6½ft (2m) orange woven ribbon, 1½in (4cm) wide*

HOW TO MAKE IT

This wreath is easy to make using a twisted stem base from a florist. I've chosen one that's made from thick grapevines twined together. Cut the stems of the poppy heads and marigolds at an angle – make each stem about 6in (15cm) long. Wire the pepperberries into small bunches *(see page 22)*. Now push the poppy and marigold stems in between the stems of the wreath base, which will hold them firmly in place. (Secure with a glue gun, if the base is loosely twined). Use strands of raffia to tie on bunches of salvia and marjoram, threading the raffia through two or three of the base stems and tying the ends into small, neat bows. Wire in the bunches of pink pepperberries by their floral-wire tails. Wind ribbon around the wreath to complete it.

• Marjoram
The variety called sweet marjoram is especially aromatic and will scent the air all around the wreath

• Marigold
Traditional, cottagey flowers like marigolds are a good choice for informal designs

Woven ribbon
Decorate your wreath with rustic binding that complements its
• *natural ingredients*

• Field poppy
The neutral shade of the seedheads helps bring the stronger colors to life

CORNFLOWER GARLAND

DELICATE GARLANDS AND FESTOONS look most attractive when they're twisted around the pole of a tent, looped along the front of a long serving table, or are used to frame a small window or doorway. If a garland is to hang free, I find it best to attach the plant material into a slender base framework of chicken wire and moss *(see page 86,* FRUITED HOLLY FESTOON*)*, because on a flexible cord base such as the one here, the heavier flowers will always turn over and flop downward.

WHAT YOU WILL NEED

FOR EVERY 39IN (1M) OF GARLAND
- *39in (1m) sturdy cord*
- *Medium-gauge floral wires*
- *Spool wire*
- *12 lychee fruits*
- *60 heads blue cornflowers*
- *15 sprigs feverfew*
- *12 stems* Protea *'Blushing Bride'*
- *15 sprigs baby's breath*
- *3 strands smilax*

HOW TO MAKE IT

This garland is made on a FLEXIBLE BASE *(see pages 24–25).*
Push a short length of floral wire into the base of each lychee fruit. Make up small bunches of all the flowers, adding the fruits as well. Bind each bunch to the cord with spool wire as you go, overlapping its head with the stems of the last. Dress any gaps with extra flowers. Twine smilax through the garland (get a friend to help with this).

Cornflower
These come also in red, pink, white, and mauve, but the familiar blue flowers are still my favorites •

Baby's breath •
This variety, 'Bristol Fairy', is a light-as-air cobweb of double white flowers held on the finest of stems

Lychee
The wonderfully textured
and colorful skin encloses
a deliciously scented, edible
• fruit with a glossy seed

Smilax
This scrambling foliage
plant is grown on fine
• strands of cotton

Protea 'Blushing Bride'
A miniature and rather
less usual form of protea,
with flowers of the most
• delicate ice pink

Feverfew
The charming flowers, which
resemble tiny chrysanthemums,
are an old herbal remedy for
• relieving aches and pains

CELOSIA SPHERES

ADD A FOCUS OF INTEREST to a simple bedroom or study with one of these intensely colorful dried flower spheres. Although they are a little time-consuming to put together, they are not at all hard to make. Choose your own combination of colors, but be sure to use a good variety of different flowers, leaves, and seedheads to give a range of shapes and textures to the finished arrangement. My raspberry-pink celosia and blackberry-colored strawflowers with steely blue globe thistles make a lively and exciting partnership.

WHAT YOU WILL NEED

FOR ONE HANGING SPHERE
- *4in (10cm) diameter dry foam sphere*
- *Medium-gauge floral wires*
- *Glue gun*
- *Reindeer moss*
- *15 maroon roses*
- *15 dark red roses*
- *15 pink miniature roses, including some buds*
- *15 miniature globe thistles*
- *5 stems purple statice (optional)*
- *10 stems pink cockscomb celosia*
- *10 stems maroon strawflowers*
- *6½ft (2m) wire-edged ribbon, 2in (5cm) wide*

HOW TO MAKE IT

Bend a 14in (35cm) floral wire in half. Push the two ends through the dry foam sphere. Cut a piece of ribbon 24in (60cm) long and thread it through the wire loop. Secure the ribbon by pulling the wire ends tight and bending them back into the base of the sphere.

Glue on reindeer moss to cover the sphere, then hang it up by the ribbon at an easy working height. Roses, globe thistles, and statice all have strong stems, so you can push them easily into the sphere. The weak-stemmed strawflowers and fat-stemmed celosia must be glued into place, though. Balance the arrangement for both color and texture, keeping an informal feel. Attach wired ribbon tails or loops to the sphere at either end.

Miniature globe thistle
The dense, compact heads are sharply spiked when dried

Miniature rose
Choose tight buds on strong stems, and include some of their leaves

Ribbon bow
A small bow at the base is an integral part of the design

Decorative tails
I made the pretty zigzag edging
of these tails by cutting the
ribbon with dressmaker's
pinking shears •

Multi-looped bow
Flamboyant bows with
perky, unfloppy loops
are easy to achieve if
you use ribbon that's
wired at the edge •

Statice •
Put in these delicate,
flowery clusters if you
want an arrangement
with a less somber look

Strawflower •
Ever popular, and
available in a huge color
range to match almost
any room scheme

Cockscomb celosia •
The soft, velvety swirls and
vivid colors of the celosia
plumes contrast with the
spiny texture and subtle
hues of the globe thistles

SWEET PEA WREATH

THERE IS NOTHING QUITE AS BEAUTIFUL as the scent of sweet peas, and no other flower perfume is quite like it. The beginning of the season, just as summer gets into full swing, is the best time for them. Then, their flowers are held on strong stalks; their blooms last a little better; and their scent is as intense as it ever gets. For this charming fresh flower wreath, I've matched sweet peas in shades of lavender with lilac-colored statice. The foliage and minuscule flowers of snow-in-summer provide bright touches of silver-green, white, and yellow. Hang the completed wreath in any setting where it can be easily seen and admired. If you are entertaining, your guests will remember, with pleasure and for many summers to come, the heady scent and subtle colors of your sweet pea wreath.

Paper ribbon •
Excellent for twirling into curls and twists that hold their shape

WHAT YOU WILL NEED

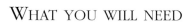

- *12in (30cm) diameter circular wet foam wreath base*
- *10 stems snow-in-summer foliage, including some flowers*
- *40 stems pale & darker lavender-colored sweet peas*
- *15 stems lilac-colored statice*
- *6½ft (2m) green & white paper ribbon, ⅜in (1cm) wide*

Sweet pea •
Lovely but short-lived, the deliciously scented sweet pea traditionally symbolizes both delicate pleasure and departure

HOW TO MAKE IT

Sweet peas last only two or three hours out of water before starting to wilt, so it is best to arrange the flowers in a wet foam base. Soak the base in water until the foam is damp through. The base will drip when hung up if you oversoak it. Trim the foliage and flower stems into sprigs about 6in (15cm) long. Put in the foliage first, spacing it evenly around the circle. Keep a few sprigs aside to fill in any gaps later on. Place the sweet peas and statice among the foliage, either in bands spiraling across the wreath, as I've done, or at random. Fill in with the foliage sprigs that you set aside, so that the foam is entirely hidden. Complete the wreath with curlicues of narrow paper ribbon.

Statice •
Paler shades, like the lilac I've chosen, suit the tissue-thin petals of statice best, though the flowers come in bolder color variants

Snow-in-summer
*Use stems with a good
mix of variegation:
the topmost leaves
have the broadest
• white margins*

SIMPLE SUNFLOWER SHAPES

FOR SPECIAL OCCASIONS, decorations that are wonderfully opulent, rich, and extravagant have a great appeal; but for everyday, it's nice to have something less outspoken up your sleeve – something with a simplicity of form and color that's comfortable to live with, yet that still holds your attention. My triangle and diamond are unfussy shapes, made from bundles of raffia-tied stems decorated with dried seedheads and flowers in woodsy colors. Hanging up in your kitchen or hallway, they make an out-of-the-ordinary decoration that will last for a year or so. Give them an occasional gentle blow with a hair dryer to keep any dust at bay.

WHAT YOU WILL NEED

FOR BOTH SUNFLOWER SHAPES
• *Natural raffia strands, for tying*
• *Glue gun*

FOR THE SUNFLOWER TRIANGLE
• *18 stems horsetail,*
12in (30cm) long, in 3 bundles
• *5 dried sunflowers*
• *10 heads craspedia*
• *2 heads leucadendron*
• *3 heads* Protea compacta
• *6 drumstick scabious seedheads,*
with bells removed from 3 of them

FOR THE SUNFLOWER DIAMOND
• *28 stems red dogwood,*
20in (50cm) long, in 4 bundles
• *9 sunflowers*
• *7 heads leucadendron*
• *9 heads* Protea mellifera
• *3 heads* Protea compacta

HOW TO MAKE THEM

Using raffia strands, bind together the bundles of stems, 1½in (4cm) or so from their ends. Cut all the flower and seedhead stalks short. Glue everything in place, pushing the glued stalks between the base stems so that they are firmly held. Cut off entirely any stalks that are too thick to push in, and glue the flower by its base onto the stems.

Craspedia
Each globular head of these saffron-colored flowers makes a bold contribution to the arrangement

Horsetail
The hard, quite rigid stems of this primitive plant are ideal for binding into a simple wreath base

Sunflower
When dried, the flower petals crinkle prettily and keep their warm, glowing color

Drumstick scabious
These seedheads look like a cluster of many little bells nestling together

Drumstick scabious
The seedheads still look good without the fragile bells

Protea mellifera
Continue the protea theme,
but don't let it get boring,
by choosing larger flowers
of a different species

Natural raffia tie
Make visible joins into
a pleasing feature of the
design by using a natural
material, like this raffia,
to bind the stems together

Protea compacta
Dried protea flowers have
"petals" with an oddly
woody appearance, and
pincushion-like centers

Leucadendron
The spiky form of these
cones is softened by the
pure white, fluffy seeds

Dogwood stems
The rich mahogany red
color of the stems is an
all-season attraction of
this cornus species

HEDGEROW WITH TREE

BRING BACK MEMORIES OF SUMMER with this stunning countryside scene, made on a mattress base and using sticks, moss, and dried flowers to create the hedgerow, gate, and tree. Do not be daunted by what may look like an ambitious project, but do set aside several hours to make it. Display the finished plaque against a wall, either sitting on a mantel or hanging like a picture. The flowers that you choose to decorate the tree canopy can suit your own color scheme. I used yarrow, a super match for my yellow dining room walls *(see pages 46–47)*.

WHAT YOU WILL NEED

FOR THE HEDGEROW
• *2 pieces chicken wire, 32in (80cm) long & 6in (15cm) wide*
• *8 handfuls dry sphagnum moss*
• *Medium-gauge floral wires, bent into hairpins 4in (10cm) long*
• *Sheet moss*
• *Bun moss*
• *Silver reindeer moss*
• *6 fronds cress seedheads*
• *6 sprigs pink campion*
• *6 drumstick scabious*
• *4 blue cornflowers*

FOR THE FRAME & GATE
• *Heavy-duty staple gun*
• *8 thin wooden struts, 4in (10cm) long*
• *Two ¾in (2cm) diameter straight branches, 39in (1m) long*
• *Four ½in (1.2cm) diameter gateposts, 4in (10cm) long, sharpened to a point at one end*
• *One ½in (1.2cm) diameter crossbar, 5in (13cm) long*

FOR THE TREE
• *1 piece chicken wire, 24in (60cm) long & 6in (15cm) wide*
• *2 handfuls dry sphagnum moss*
• *One 1¼in (3cm) diameter branched trunk, 12in (30cm) long*
• *6 handfuls green Spanish moss*
• *5 large heads yarrow, divided into several small florets*

HOW TO MAKE IT

This wall hanging is made on a MATTRESS BASE *(see pages 30–31)*. Make two moss-filled mattresses for the hedgerow. Screw the eight struts to the two straight branches to form a frame, leaving a gap of

Cress
Let tall stalks peep up over the hedge •

Bun moss
Creates a splendid 3-D effect •

7in (18cm) for the gate. Staple a hedge at each end. Screw on the four upright gateposts, then the diagonal crossbar. Attach all the plant material with wire hairpins. Make a moss-filled mattress for the tree canopy and staple it to the trunk. Screw to a hedge through the frame. Attach Spanish moss and yarrow to the tree canopy with wire hairpins.

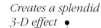

Spanish moss
The kind I've used
has been dyed a
soft green •

Yarrow florets
Dress the tree canopy
• with vivid flowers

**Pink campion
flowers**
Include spots of
• a pale color

Drumstick scabious
Clustered seedheads
• add a new texture

Tree trunk •
This branched piece
of mahonia makes
an interesting stem

Blue cornflower
Brings vitality to the
muted shades •

Sheet moss
A good material
for cladding •

Silver reindeer moss •
Pin a mossy grass verge at the hedge base

HEDGEROW WITH TREE

Dreaming up excitingly new, different things to do with plants is a satisfying aspect of working with such versatile materials. For this wall hanging, I took some familiar dried ingredients, added basic craft skills and equipment (a handful of screws, a screwdriver, a heavy-duty staple gun), and created a picture that will last for months and is easily adapted to your own design. Not a bit out of place in this English country setting, the terra-cotta figures are by Mrs. Brown, from the island of Nevis in the West Indies.

You'll find detailed instructions for making this dried flower picture on pages 44 and 45.

Lily Wedding Circlets

Choosing the colors for wedding bouquets and headdresses can be a taxing matter, as fashions change from pastels to primaries to tones of a single color. You have only to look at great paintings, or indeed great gardens, to see how well many different combinations of colors can work, both likely and unlikely ones. But the fashion for cream or ivory bridal dresses seems to endure, and this is fortunate, since with a dress in this color range, almost any flowers will look just right. In these circlets for a bride and young bridesmaid, soft pink and coral blend with yellow, and are set off by hues of green. Don't forget a blue flower, for good luck, in the bride's circlet.

What you will need

For the bride's circlet
- *Few heavy-gauge floral wires, joined to measurement of head circumference plus ¾in (2cm)*
- *Floral tape*
- *Fine spool wire*
- *5 stems berried ruscus*
- *6 houttuynia leaves*
- *5 stems yellow alstroemeria*
- *5 stems pink & white lisianthus*
- *1 borage flower*

For the bridesmaid's circlet
- *Twisted stem circle & glue gun*
- *5 trails creeping Jenny*
- *6 houttuynia leaves*
- *5 stems yellow roses*
- *3 stems coral Guernsey lilies*

How to make them

The bride's circlet is made on a Flexible Base *(see pages 24–25)*. Bind the wire base with tape, and form a round eye at one end of it. Using spool wire, attach bunches of leaves and flowers to the base. Cover the binding wire with tape before attaching the next bunch. Fasten the end through the eye. For the bridesmaid's circlet, glue everything onto the stem circle.

Guernsey lily •
The frilly petals of this nerine variety curl back to reveal slender stamens of the same color

Twisted stem circle
The bridesmaid's circlet has a ready-made base of intertwined vines

Creeping Jenny •
Trails of tiny leaves add accents of pale greeny gold

Yellow rose •
Rosa 'Landia' has small flowers and a wonderful perfume

Borage
Signifying courage, this
herb has delicate, star-
shaped blue flowers

Ruscus
Choose stems
with berries on
them, if possible

Houttuynia 'Chamaeleon'
When crushed, the leaves
release the pungent scent
of bitter oranges

Alstroemeria
These flowers last
well out of water,
so are ideal for a
bridal circlet

Lisianthus
Use a mix of open flowers
with pastel-edged petals,
and pure white buds

Wheatfield Bundles

It is easy to forget just how beautiful wheat sheaves can look, particularly now that they are no longer a commonplace sight, standing, regimented, in newly harvested fields. These two arrangements are quite easy to make, since they are really nothing more complicated than large bundles of stalks that fan out above and below a tie. On a small scale, and with the addition of a few dried flowers that look as if they could be growing wild in a wheatfield, they make an informal but still extremely picturesque wall hanging. The braided raffia ties that go around the bundles complement the natural feel of the plant material.

Cluster-flowered everlasting
Helichrysum italicum *is a variety of strawflower that has numerous small heads of woolly blooms*

What You Will Need

For the small bundle
- *Twine, for tying*
- *Fine spool wire*
- *¾in (2cm) thick bunch natural raffia, 39in (1m) long*
- *Few extra natural raffia strands, for tying braid*
- *160 stalks cone wheat*
- *7 stems yellow cluster-flowered everlasting*
- *10 stems red miniature spray roses*

For the large bundle
- *Twine, for tying*
- *Fine spool wire*
- *1½in (4cm) thick bunch natural raffia, 49in (1.25m) long*
- *Few extra natural raffia strands, for tying braid*
- *400 stalks cone wheat*
- *15 love-in-a-mist seedheads*
- *7 stems blue delphinium*
- *10 stems red miniature spray roses*

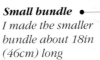

Small bundle
I made the smaller bundle about 18in (46cm) long

How To Make Them

The two bundles are made in the same way. First, braid the bunch of natural raffia. Bunch together a big handful of wheat stalks, with the heads layered down the sides a little, adding a few flower sprigs as you go. Tie three times: below the ears; in the middle; and 4in (10cm) from the base. Now layer in more wheat and flowers, tying in their stems about two-thirds of the way down. Fan out the stems at the base. Cut level. Tie a braid in a bow around the bundle, and secure its center with a raffia tie.

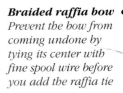

Braided raffia bow
Prevent the bow from coming undone by tying its center with fine spool wire before you add the raffia tie

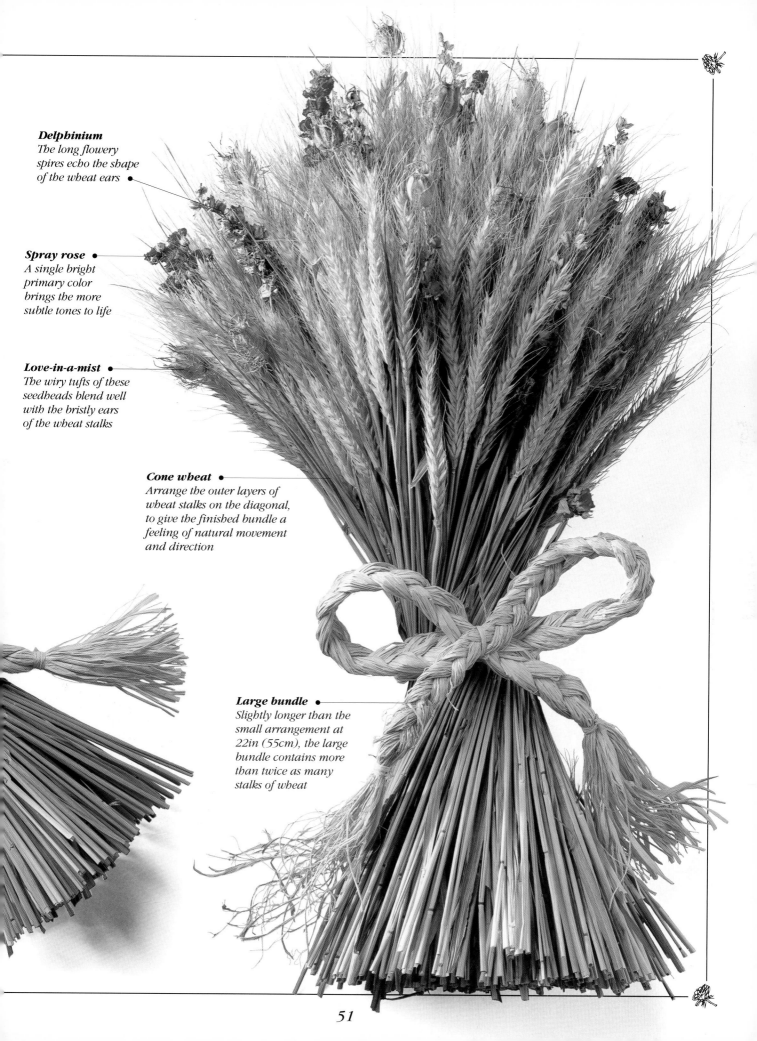

Delphinium
The long flowery spires echo the shape of the wheat ears

Spray rose
A single bright primary color brings the more subtle tones to life

Love-in-a-mist
The wiry tufts of these seedheads blend well with the bristly ears of the wheat stalks

Cone wheat
Arrange the outer layers of wheat stalks on the diagonal, to give the finished bundle a feeling of natural movement and direction

Large bundle
Slightly longer than the small arrangement at 22in (55cm), the large bundle contains more than twice as many stalks of wheat

CANDYSTRIPE GARLAND

COLORS AND TEXTURES are all-important when you are planning fresh flower garlands for a grand occasion. Because garlands often have to compete with an array of other visual delights (and especially if they are to be seen by and through a host of people, maybe at a wedding or big party), I like to choose a combination of delicate as well as bold flowers and leaves for them. Here, small bunches of stripy pink and white flowers – sweet-scented roses and carnations, pink-veined salvia, and single alstroemeria – stand out colorfully against the dense, feathery foliage of tree asparagus, wispy green heads of love-in-a-mist, and silvery eucalyptus disks.

WHAT YOU WILL NEED

FOR EVERY 39IN (1M) OF GARLAND
- *39in (1m) sturdy cord*
- *Medium-gauge floral wires*
- *Spool wire*
- *5 stems pink & white alstroemeria flowers*
- *12 pink & white zebra roses*
- *10 pink & white carnations*
- *5 stems green love-in-a-mist*
- *6 stems* Salvia horminum
- *8 stems silver gum eucalyptus*
- *12 stems tree asparagus*

HOW TO MAKE IT

This dainty garland is made on a FLEXIBLE BASE *(see pages 24–25).* Start off by wiring single flowers of the alstroemeria *(see page 22),* and the roses and carnations *(see page 23).* Make up small, mixed bunches of all the wired flowers, including sprigs of love-in-a-mist, salvia, eucalyptus, and plenty of tree asparagus in each one. Bind each bunch to the base cord with reel wire as you make it, so that its head overlaps the stems of the previous bunch. Fill in gaps with any remaining flowers and leaves.

Silver gum
This eucalyptus species has oval leaves of a beautiful dusky blue

Tree asparagus
The spires of feathery foliage are perfect for filling out garlands

Love-in-a-mist
Choose a variety
with green flowers,
as I have, or one in
blue or white •

Salvia horminum
Pale pink bracts,
veined in a deeper
hue, surround the
• tiny flowers

Zebra rose •
Crushed raspberry-
pink stripes mottle
the petals of this
unusual cultivar

Carnation •
The scent of cloves
gives these flowers
a spicy fragrance

• **Alstroemeria**
Spots and stripes
provide delicate
splashes of color

LARKSPUR RAFFIA RING

A SIMPLE AND HOMEY-LOOKING ring made of dried country flowers and seedcases is just right for hanging against the natural wood of an unpainted door, or on one of the inner walls of a sheltered patio, where it will be protected from the weather. The base of this wreath is a thick raffia braid, joined into a circle. A decorative, thinner braided bow covers the join of the two ends. To blend with the biscuity tones of the raffia, I've chosen strawflowers of a somewhat paler color, together with larkspur in two subtle shades of blue, spiky gray-blue globe thistle heads, and fronds of pale green shepherd's purse. The flowers spray out from the ring of braided raffia in an exuberant swirl, like sparks flying from a spinning Catherine wheel.

WHAT YOU WILL NEED

- *1 thick bunch natural raffia, 59in (1.5m) long*
- *1 thin bunch natural raffia, 30in (75cm) long*
- *Medium-gauge floral wires*
- *25 stems lavender-blue larkspur*
- *25 stems navy blue larkspur*
- *25 stems ivory strawflowers*
- *45 longish sprigs shepherd's purse fronds*
- *20 heads miniature globe thistle*

Shepherd's purse •
Arrange the seedcase fronds with the flowers so that they hang free around the ring in a clockwise direction

Larkspur •
This lovely cottage-garden plant dries extremely well, and you can grow dwarf forms in containers if you have no garden

HOW TO MAKE IT

This large wreath is made on a RIGID BASE *(see page 27, MAKING A BRAIDED RAFFIA RING)*.
The base for this circle needs to be quite substantial, so that it will hold its shape without drooping when the flowers are in and the wreath is hung up. Use the long raffia bunch to make a braid 2½in (6cm) thick. Join the ends to form a circle 15in (38cm) in diameter.

Make a narrow braid with the thin bunch of raffia and tie into a bow. Bind the bow over the join of the circle with a raffia strand or two. Set aside a few stems of larkspur. Make up small bunches of all the remaining plant material *(see page 22)*. Push the wire of each bunch into the base, securing and hiding it inside the raffia strands. Fill any gaps with the remaining larkspur.

The finished ring
Hung out of bright light, this dried flower arrangement will last and look good for many months

Miniature globe thistle
The spiky round heads make a nice visual contrast with the flowing larkspur spires and fronds of shepherd's purse •

Strawflower
A soft shade of white brightens the deeper colors but doesn't jar against them

EXOTIC WALL BASKET

FINDING THE IDEAL PLACE to display arrangements of flowers for special occasions is not always easy. Side tables must be cleared away to make standing room for guests, and all the space on the dining table is often taken up with food. Wall baskets solve such dilemmas, because they can be hung up on the wall like paintings, anywhere you like. The exotic *mélange* of flowers that fills this wire vegetable half-basket includes the highly scented tuberose. Its pervasive, spicily sweet fragrance will fill the largest of rooms within moments.

WHAT YOU WILL NEED

- *10in (25cm) diameter wire mesh half-basket*
- *3 double handfuls damp sphagnum or sheet moss*
- *Sturdy plastic trash bag*
- *3 bricks wet foam, well soaked*
- *9 stems tuberose*
- *5 stems gloriosa lilies*
- *3 stems green anthurium*
- *1 stem deep yellow Cymbidium orchids*
- *10 stems greeny yellow miniature Singapore orchids*
- *3 stems pink miniature Singapore orchids*
- *3 stems mahonia leaves*
- *5 stems purplish leucadendron*
- *5 large poplar or other leaves*

Gloriosa lily foliage •
This climbing plant uses the ends of its leaves as tendrils

Poplar leaf
Choose any leaves that are large and broad enough to balance the linearity of the gloriosa lily and mahonia foliage •

HOW TO MAKE IT

Use any sort of half-basket that is suitable to plant up and hang on an outside wall. For a wire mesh basket, first line all except its flat back with damp moss. Then line the entire basket with plastic. Cut pieces of soaked wet foam to fill the pocket: make them fit snugly.

Hang your basket in its final place (or stand it in another container to hold it firmly upright) and arrange the plant material in the wet foam. Keep the arrangement informal, so that the flowers seem to spring up from the center of the basket, like water gushing out of a fountain.

Tuberose
Use with care, because
the strong scent is not
• always welcome

Miniature orchid
For longer-lasting blooms,
stand the orchid stems in
deep water for a few hours
before you make the basket

Anthurium
A green form of these
usually red, odd
flowers adds a
• novel touch

Leucadendron
These leathery leaves
are produced by an
• evergreen shrub

Cymbidium orchid
You can get this "queen of
exotic flowers" in almost
every color except blue

Gloriosa lily flower
The wavy-edged petals
and dancing stamens
make the flowers look
especially graceful

Mahonia leaf
Each leaflet lobe ends in a vicious spike,
so be careful how you handle these leaves

INGENIOUS WIRE RING

UNDERSTATED ELEGANCE AND SIMPLICITY are the hallmarks of this copper and gold circular garland, which looks equally good in formal and informal settings. Find a plain-colored wall to display it against, because like most unframed wall hangings, it would tend to be lost against a very busy wallpaper. To my mind, this garland has the appearance of something both ancient and precious, and it would suit a contemporary location particularly well. When acorns are in season, I would gild and add just a few, to enhance the oak leaves. One note of caution: if your household includes cats, don't hang the garland any place within their reach, for feathers are like ambrosia to cats, and they could easily destroy your creation in moments.

WHAT YOU WILL NEED

- *39in (1m) lightweight electrical copper-wire cable*
- *39in (1m) heavy-duty electrical copper-wire cable*
- *Gold spray paint*
- *Strong multi-purpose glue*
- *25 pressed oak or beech leaves*
- *10 duck or other feathers*

Copper-wire tendril •
When coiling the wire for the tendrils, wind it very tightly around the pencil, but extend each coil more or less to get tendrils of a varying springiness

Duck feather •
I got these free from my local friendly fishseller, but you could use any feathers that suit the restrained tone of the other ingredients in the ring

HOW TO MAKE IT

Start by stripping away the casing of the lightweight electrical cable. Separate the copper wires inside and lay them straight. Strip off the casing of the heavy-duty wire, but unwind the wires gently to keep their wavy curves intact. Spray the oak leaves with gold paint. Make the nine curly tendrils by winding 12in (30cm) lengths of the finer wire around a thin round pencil. Leave a straight end of 2in (5cm), and extend the spiral slightly as you pull each of the tendrils off the pencil. Loosely bend five of the heavy wires into a ring 15in (38cm) in diameter, so that their ends just overlap. Weave in three more wires to form the three free ends. Use the finer wire to tie off any joins. Bind the tendrils to the ring by their straight ends. Finally, attach the leaves and feathers in position with spots of strong glue.

Gilded leaf
Spray the leaves a rich gold
on the top side only, letting
the natural leaf color show
through in some places as
I did, or on both sides

Copper-wire free end
Where leaves and feathers
are glued on, don't try to
hide any joins – just see
the leaf stems as part of
the decoration

Pressed oak leaf
Look for leaves on
countryside rambles
or walks in the park,
and then press them
between two books
to dry them out

Jaunty Garland

Mostly, I like to use flowers in their own growing season, but there are times, particularly in the middle of winter, when it's comforting to know that year-round varieties are still available in all colors of the rainbow. With its combination of seasonless flowers, this vivid garland could be made at almost any time of year. Gerberas, roses, and orchids all come in a host of colors that will allow you to match the mood of your garland to its location. My zingy orange and pink scheme is continued in the jaunty starfish and spirals of rich pink ribbon. Balance the strength of the other colors with leaves in a bold green.

Mexican orange blossom
The foliage of this evergreen shrub is sweetly aromatic

Dried starfish
Use an electric drill at slow speed (or a hand drill) fitted with a fine bit to make tiny holes in the starfish for the gold hanging threads

Galax
With their uncomplicated shape, strong color, and fine network of veining, galax leaves provide the perfect background and foil for the flowers

Miniature orchid
Finding flowers so like the starfish was a stroke of luck!

WHAT YOU WILL NEED

FOR EVERY 39IN (1M) OF GARLAND
- *39in (1m) sturdy cord*
- *Medium-gauge floral wires*
- *Spool wire*
- *12 pink gerbera flowers*
- *5 peach-pink roses*
- *5 green Cymbidium orchids*
- *5 stems each orange & deep pink miniature Singapore orchids*
- *20 galax leaves*
- *15 sprigs variegated ivy*
- *10 sprigs Mexican orange blossom foliage*
- *10 orange dried starfish, strung with metallic gold thread*
- *10ft (3m) shocking pink wire-edged ribbon, 1½in (4cm) wide*

HOW TO MAKE IT

This garland is made on a FLEXIBLE BASE *(see pages 24–25)*.
Start by wiring short stems of the gerbera flowers, the roses, and all the orchids *(see page 23)*. Make up small bunches of these wired flowers, together with pieces of the foliage. Bind each bunch to the cord with spool wire as you make it, so that its head overlaps the stalks of the previous bunch.

If the garland is to hang against a table *(see pages 62–63)*, use fine tacks to secure it to the top edge in scallops. Fasten the scallops to the cloth with safety pins pushed through from back to front. Fill in with extra flowers to beautify the garland, then hang the starfish by their gold threads. Spiral ribbon through, and add a multi-looped bow at the apex of each scallop.

Cymbidium orchid
Lime green adds unexpected visual accents to my flower theme of pink and orange

Variegated ivy
Creamy foliage prevents the garland from looking too dense and heavy

Gerbera
Equally versatile for special and everyday arrangements, these daisy-like flowers are available throughout the year as large or miniature blooms, in a choice of jolly, vivacious colors

Rose
Choose small, tight buds that will open in the heat of a warm room

JAUNTY GARLAND

*Weddings and anniversaries;
a college graduation; the
birth of a child: the lives of
our families and bosom
friends are punctuated with
landmark events that seem as
if tailor-made for celebrating
in exuberant style. Add a
touch of magic to the
occasion, and make it one
always to remember, by
garlanding not just serving
tables, but window- and
door-frames too, with
sumptuously ribbon-decked
festoons of dazzling fresh
flowers and brilliant foliage.*

You'll find detailed instructions
for making this fresh flower
garland on pages 60 and 61.

CALENDULA HEART

WHAT COULD BE MORE WELCOMING for an anniversary or birthday celebration in high summer than a simple heart of flowers hanging on the front door, where it will be seen by each one of your guests the minute they arrive. If you have a garden, then this is the time of year when it's ablaze with flowers that echo the colors and feel of sunshine and unclouded skies; and summer is especially the season to enjoy sweet cottagey flowers, like the delphiniums and calendulas that I've chosen for my heart-shaped wreath. Don't be fearful of combining flowers with jazzily contrasting colors: just pack them close together to your own design, and let them work their wonders.

Globe amaranth
The dense, cloverlike heads of flowers are produced from summer through to the early autumn, and keep their rich colors – red, orange, purple, pink, or white – when dried

Calendula
Sunny calendulas, also called pot marigolds, have been cultivated in English cottage gardens since the late sixteenth century

WHAT YOU WILL NEED

- *17in (43cm) diameter heart-shaped wet foam wreath base*
- *60 tips* Euonymus fortunei *'Emerald and Gold'*
- *20 stems calendulas*
- *20 heads red globe amaranth*
- *20 stems* Chrysanthemum carinatum *'Monarch Court Jesters'*
- *2 stems blue delphinium*
- *6½ft (2m) pink & white wire-edged ribbon, 1¼in (3cm) wide*

HOW TO MAKE IT

Soak the wet foam wreath base in water until the foam has taken up enough water to be damp all the way through. Do not oversoak it, though, or the base will be heavy and also drip when it is hung up. Cut all of the foliage and flowers, except the delphinium stems, into pieces 3in (7.5cm) long. Separate the delphinium stems into florets.

First, put in the tips of variegated euonymus. Arrange the foliage at an angle, and running in a single direction around the heart. Put in the calendulas next, spacing them unevenly, but keeping a balanced feel to the arrangement. Now put in some clusters as well as single heads of globe amaranth flowers. Place the chrysanthemums, again keeping a good balance between the different color tones. Finally, tuck florets of blue delphinium in among the other flowers. Cut the ribbon into short lengths of about 6in (15cm) or so, and spiral them in around the flowers and foliage.

Euonymus
Use foliage with a golden
variegation that picks up
the brilliant yellow of the
chrysanthemums and
• calendula flowers

• **Chrysanthemum**
Look again if you think
chrysanthemum means
autumnal oranges and
browns: each daisy head
of 'Monarch Court Jesters'
sports three lively colors
and a starburst center

• **Delphinium**
I chose the intensely colored
'Blue Bee' so that the single
florets – though small and
delicate – really sing out

LOTS OF PODS

SOME SEEDS AND PODS have fascinating shapes that can be used to cunning advantage in many sorts of arrangements. This wall-mounted plaque has something about it that calls to mind an armorial shield. It combines clusters of tropical seedheads and pods, arranged in a random yet symmetrical oval pattern, with bundles of wheat. A rich blue and gold Napoleonic silk ribbon binds the stalks of wheat and forms a decorative cockade at the intersection of the bundles. With such an ornate ribbon, this creation would do justice to a formal dining or sitting room. A simpler ribbon, perhaps a tartan one, is a better choice for casual settings.

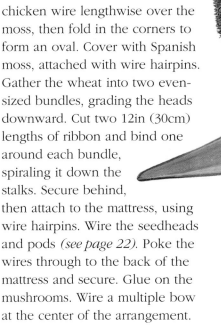

Wheat stalks •
The smooth, not whiskery, ears of bread wheat suit the clean lines and firm forms of this bold design

Tropical seedpod
Look for exotic varieties like this wherever dried flowers are the specialty, and also in some home design shops •

Tropical seedhead
Buy as great a selection of shapes and textures as you can get hold of •

WHAT YOU WILL NEED

- *1 piece chicken wire, 30in (75cm) long & 12in (30cm) wide*
- *9 handfuls dry sphagnum moss*
- *Medium-gauge floral wires, some bent into hairpins 4in (10cm) long*
- *Spool wire & glue gun*
- *4 large handfuls natural undyed Spanish moss*
- *80 wheat stalks*
- *50–60 assorted tropical dried seedheads & pods*
- *5 large dried mushroom cones*
- *6½ft (2m) wire-edged silk or other ribbon, 2in (5cm) wide*

HOW TO MAKE IT

This wall hanging is made on a MATTRESS BASE *(see pages 30–31)*. Make an oval mattress of moss-filled chicken wire. Place a layer of moss on one half of the piece of chicken wire. Make it as wide as the chicken wire, 15in (38cm) long, and 1in (2.5cm) or so thick. Fold the other half of the piece of chicken wire lengthwise over the moss, then fold in the corners to form an oval. Cover with Spanish moss, attached with wire hairpins. Gather the wheat into two even-sized bundles, grading the heads downward. Cut two 12in (30cm) lengths of ribbon and bind one around each bundle, spiraling it down the stalks. Secure behind, then attach to the mattress, using wire hairpins. Wire the seedheads and pods *(see page 22)*. Poke the wires through to the back of the mattress and secure. Glue on the mushrooms. Wire a multiple bow at the center of the arrangement.

Dried mushroom
*The cones are thin
• and very fragile*

• Spanish moss
*Cladding the base with moss
gives the edges an attractive
finish and ensures that no
patches of chicken wire are
visible in the arrangement*

AUTUMN BRIDAL RING

THE MUTED FLOWERS OF HYDRANGEA and globe amaranth, and the fluffy seedheads of wild clematis, encircle a twig frame of willow canes in this mellow wreath. A charming alternative to the more usual bridal bouquet, the ring is light and easy to carry on the day, and can be dried afterward to make a sweet keepsake. This adventurous creation, which would be lovely for a wedding in the autumn, looks very special against an ivory and gold dress. Complete the bridal picture with a twig headdress, and miniature rings of the same flowers for the bridesmaids to carry.

WHAT YOU WILL NEED

- *10 thin willow canes, 59in (1.5m) long*
- *Glue gun*
- *30 small hydrangea florets, in mixed pinks, blues, & greens*
- *30 globe amaranth flowers, in shades of warm pink & coral*
- *8 long trails wild clematis*
- *6½ft (2m) blue & gold silk ribbon, 1½in (4cm) wide*

HOW TO MAKE IT

Entwine the supple willow canes, joining the ends to make a circle 12in (30cm) in diameter. Glue all the hydrangea florets and globe amaranth flowers onto the circle, leaving a space at the top to form the handle. Cut the wild clematis trails into short lengths. Use small dabs of glue to attach them here and there among the flowers. Fill in the plant material on one side, with the ring lying flat, then hang it up and fill in the back, for both sides will be on display. Bind the top space with ribbon, and attach flowing ribbon tails to the handle.

Hydrangea •
Use a domed, mop-headed variety, which will furnish you with a very generous number of small florets from each large head

Silk ribbon tails •
Ideally, your choice of ribbon should be as extravagant as the budget allows: gorgeous ribbon like this won't be a bargain, but any important event is worth some expense

Covered handle
Ribbon wound around
this part of the entwined
willow-cane base provides
a decorative finish and a
more comfortable handle

Globe amaranth
You may need to hunt a bit
for these striking shades of
warm pink, since they're
more unusual than the
clear, bright colors

Wild clematis
Lovely country names for this
plant are old man's beard or
traveler's joy, evoking a long
life with moments of rapture
for one partner (at least) of
the newly married twosome

RUSTIC BUNCHES

SIMPLE CREATIONS ARE EVERY BIT as effective as the more elaborate arrangements, and you can make a pretty decoration for your home just by hanging bunches of dried flowers against a wall or on a door. Your own choice of color scheme for the flowers and foliage should work well with the place in which the bunches will hang, but need not be a slavish match to the surroundings. The two bunches that I've put together here both use the silvery foliage of artemisia, but with different flowers in the same color range of peach, orange, and red, each has a unique and special charm. Finish the bunches with rustic ribbons, and hang them out of strong sunlight.

WHAT YOU WILL NEED

FOR THE SMALL BUNCH
• *Twine, for tying*
• *10 stems artemisia foliage*
• *15 stems red roses*
• *15 stems orange strawflowers*
• *10 heads safflower*
• *39in (1m) gray-green grosgrain ribbon, 1½in (4cm) wide*

FOR THE LARGE BUNCH
• *Twine, for tying*
• *10 stems artemisia foliage*
• *25 stems peach-pink roses*
• *20 stems red bottlebrush*
• *39in (1m) peach-pink grosgrain ribbon, 1½in (4cm) wide*

HOW TO MAKE THEM

These bunches are both made in the same very easy way. Start off by putting together a narrow fan of the longest stems of artemisia foliage, roses, strawflowers, and safflower heads (or bottlebrush). This fixes the shape of the bunch. Now layer in the remaining plant material, making sure that there are flowers and foliage almost as far as the point at which the bow will be attached. Bind the bunch firmly around with twine, tying it 4in (10cm) or so from the ends of the stems. Cut 12in (30cm) from the length of ribbon. Tie the rest into a double bow, and attach to the bunch with the short length.

Strawflower
This well-known everlasting is popular everywhere, easy to find in almost any place that sells dried flowers, and usually good value besides

Rose
Even when dried, deeply scented varieties retain a vestige of fragrance that reminds us of their sweet, full-blown summer glory

Safflower
The tufty, thistlelike heads of safflower yield a bright orange-yellow dye, giving the plant its traditional name of dyer's saffron

Uneven stems
I think the informality of a not-too-even finish is quite charming, but you could cut the stem ends level if you're keen on neatness

Ribbon bow with tails
The closely ribbed weave of grosgrain ribbon suits the rough textures of the dried plant ingredients

Bottlebrush
Native to all parts of Australia, the many species of bottlebrush (Callistemon) have numerous colorful and slender stamens, which surround the stem in clusters of soft spikes

Artemisia
Use these feathery stems of pleasantly aromatic, gray-green foliage as a single, unifying theme that flows through the two separate bunches

GALA SWAG

Globe artichoke
The tightly closed buds have a sculptural look that contrasts sharply with the magnificent open flowerheads

Heather
Trailing bunches of bell heather encourage the naturally downward direction of the swag

COLOR PLAYS A CONSIDERABLE PART in our everyday lives. It conjures atmospheres, affects our mood, and provides us with all manner of associations. This gloriously rich swag would be a wonderful decoration for an autumn wedding party. Even though there is something about the mood of its color scheme that reminds me instantly of autumn, the swag doesn't contain the colors that are usually associated with that time of year – those dusky rusts, reds, and oranges that I think are a little somber for such a joyous occasion as a wedding. Rather, it combines a toothsome range of pinks that runs from the deep lilac-pink of the globe artichoke flowers to the orange-pink of the celosia. Pink-budded viburnum strikes a vibrant chord, and clumps of heather bring abundant good luck.

Viburnum
In autumn, this evergreen shrub (also called laurustinus) offers you a quartet of delights: glossy green leaves, pink buds, white flowers, and blue berry-fruits shaped as tiny ovals

• **Cockscomb celosia**
Despite its exotic appearance, this plant is no bother to grow, and the squiggly, soft, almost irresistibly touchable flower plumes add richness to any arrangement at a stroke

WHAT YOU WILL NEED

• *1 piece chicken wire, 65in (165cm) long & 8in (20cm) wide*
• *20 handfuls sphagnum moss*
• *Medium-gauge floral wires*
• *Spool wire*
• *30 sprigs deep pink heather*
• *12 globe artichoke flowers*
• *10 stems cockscomb celosia, in shades of pink & orange-pink*
• *60 sprigs viburnum foliage with flowers, some in bud*

HOW TO MAKE IT

This swag is made on a RIGID BASE *(see page 26,* MAKING A CIRCULAR CHICKEN WIRE AND MOSS BASE). Roll the chicken wire around the moss for the base. Bend to shape. Wire bunches of heather, single artichoke flowers, and pieces of celosia *(see page 22).* Leave each with a 6in (15cm) floral-wire end. Push sprigs of viburnum into the base to cover its front, then wire in the flowers. Give everything a fluid movement down to the base of the loop and the two tail ends.

THE EPITOME OF SUMMER

EARLY SUMMER IS A MAGICAL TIME of the year – the time when most of our favorite flowers are in their prime. Peonies, sweet peas, roses, lilies, ranunculus, delphiniums: of all flowers, these are among the most sumptuous, and not only for their looks – many are also lusciously scented. This ring epitomizes the mood of summer perfectly, its shades of pink set off by gold-green foliage and twinkles of sharp yellow. Here are great fat peonies, their sweet scent and cupped petals mixing with the spicy fragrance and calm beauty of the lily trumpets. Spires of deep red orchids and peachily pink ranunculus, like miniature peonies, appear among these more showy flowers, with deft touches of yellow kangaroo paw that enliven the softer colors. For a summer treat, invite favored friends to dine outside, and set this lovely ring close to the table.

Vanda orchid •
Arrange the spires so that some longer stems with buds are mingled among shorter clusters of full-blown blossoms

WHAT YOU WILL NEED

• *12in (30cm) diameter circular wet foam wreath base*
• *5 stems eucalyptus foliage*
• *8 pink peonies*
• *10 white & pink oriental lilies*
• *10 stems pink ranunculus*
• *10 stems deep burgundy red Vanda orchids*
• *3 stems yellow kangaroo paw*

Kangaroo paw •
The white flowers of this native Australian plant are completely enclosed at first by their slender, felted yellow sepals

HOW TO MAKE IT

You can buy wet foam bases in good flower shops and in many garden centers. Begin by soaking the base according to the maker's instructions. The foam should be damp through. Do not oversoak it, or the base will be very heavy and also drip when it is hung up. Arrange the plant material clockwise above the center of the ring

and counterclockwise below. Put in sprigs of the eucalyptus foliage first, then the peonies, arranging the heads at random. Because lily pollen stains, remove the stamens before arranging the flowers into the ring. Put groups of ranunculus at both the outer and inner edges, interspersed with pieces of orchid and a sprinkle of kangaroo paw.

Eucalyptus •
Unless you specially like its pungent scent, choose young foliage that is not too aromatic, or go for the species known as lemon-scented gum

Ranunculus
*This flower belongs to
the same plant family
as the lowly buttercup
and ethereal peony*

Peony
*I love these gorgeous,
silken-petaled blooms,
and their brief season
makes them seem even
more precious*

Oriental lily
*The creamy flutes
of Lilium 'Pompeii'
reveal dainty pink
markings as they
unfold and open*

MELLOW HOP SWAG

AUTUMN ARRIVES, AND ONCE MORE the color spectrum changes, from the clear, bright tones of summer to the warm baked-earth colors of the setting sun and of smoky bonfires. Embrace this transition into the new season, and celebrate the good feel of autumn, with a garland of dried hop flowers, yarrow, golden strawflowers, rusty cress seedheads, and ruby chilies, all intertwined with loops of tawny paper ribbon. The green of the hops highlights the duskier hues, making the whole garland glow.

WHAT YOU WILL NEED

FOR EVERY 39IN (1M) OF GARLAND
- *39in (1m) sturdy cord*
- *Spool wire*
- *6 bunches cress seedheads*
- *15 sprigs hop flowers*
- *6 stems yarrow*
- *20 stems yellow strawflowers*
- *15 red preserved chilies*
- *6½ft (2m) coiled paper ribbon*

HOW TO MAKE IT

This chunky garland is made on a FLEXIBLE BASE *(see pages 24–25).* Cut the paper ribbon into 12in (30cm) lengths and fan them out. Make up bunches of all the plant material, wiring in the chilies and loops of ribbon as well. Bind the bunches onto the cord with spool wire as you make them, attaching the few back stems of each bunch to those of the bunch it overlaps. This keeps the garland together, and makes it easier to hang. Add some extra flowers and ribbon loops once it's hung in place.

Cress
These airy fronds, which vary in tone from greenish brown through to russet red, have a pleasantly crunchy feel and texture that creates a perfect background for the other plant ingredients

Yarrow
'Coronation Gold' *is a
cultivar of the species*
Achillea filipendulina,
*which has an
exceptional
color and
dries well* •

Strawflower
*Choose heads of the
deepest gold that
you can find*

Preserved chili
*These can sting skin as much
as fresh ones, so wash your
hands after handling them*

• **Hop**
*Only female plants produce
these drooping clusters of
conelike flower bracts*

Paper ribbon •
*The compact coils look a
bit unpromising but are
easy to stretch out*

MELLOW HOP SWAG

Everyone has a favorite season, and if autumn is yours, I feel sure you'll love the evocative, bittersweet color palette of this quickly made swag. Its deep reds and golden yellows recall the hazy heat of summer, and bronze seedheads tell of bare winter earth, but the fragile green hop flowers remind us that spring will follow before long. Drape your swag around a log-filled fireplace, or twine it down a staircase, as I did: either way, it'll look glorious.

You'll find detailed instructions for making this dried flower swag on pages 76 and 77.

HOT CHILI BONANZA

HANG THIS TWISTED STEM CIRCLE of pods, berries, and flowers on your front door as a brilliant beacon to greet a group of close friends arriving at an autumn harvest or Thanksgiving party. You can be sure that the festivities will get off to a lively start. All the plant material that I've put together for this wreath is fresh, except for the orange safflower heads, and will last well. Even when the chili peppers and strands of bittersweet and privet berries have shriveled, the ring will still have an attractively faded appeal. The color range brings to this arrangement all the rich tones of autumn, through yellow to orange, red, and inky black; and, of course, autumn is the prime time for finding the ingredients.

WHAT YOU WILL NEED

- *22in (55cm) diameter ready-made twisted stem circle* or
- *10 thin willow or hazel canes, 59in (1.5m) long*
- *Fine spool wire*
- *Glue gun*
- *3 stems each green, yellow, & red chilies*
- *5 stems round orange chilies*
- *3 stems berried privet*
- *5 stems bittersweet*
- *30 heads dried safflower*

Bittersweet •
This twining climber is grown especially for its beautiful red and yellow fruits

Privet •
Arrange the glossy black berries in small clusters and some larger clumps around the circle

HOW TO MAKE IT

You can buy twig or stem wreath bases similar to the one I've used here in most good flower shops and many garden centers, or you could try making one yourself. To do this, take four or five of the willow or hazel canes. Twist and bend them together into a circle roughly 22in (55cm) in diameter. Overlap the ends and secure with fine spool wire. Weave in the rest of the canes to build up the base.

Secure them into the twisted base layer by threading and spiraling them through the existing canes. Trim all the plant material so that each piece measures 6in (15cm) long or so. Tuck the chilies into the base first, wedging their stalks firmly in between the overlapping canes. Put in strands of privet and bittersweet berries. Finally, put in the safflowers. Glue on any short pieces that cannot be wedged in.

Serrano chili •
Select stems of these very hot red chili peppers with a few unripe green pods

Cascabel chili
This variety gets its name from
● a Spanish word for rattle

Safflower ●
The strange thistlelike heads
retain their wonderfully sunny
orange-gold color when dried

Jalapeño pepper
Originally from Mexico,
these fiery chilies are
● also good pickled

● **Szechuan chili**
The elegant yellow pods
are edible, as are all the
chilies that adorn this
twisted stem circle

WINTER-WHITE SWAG

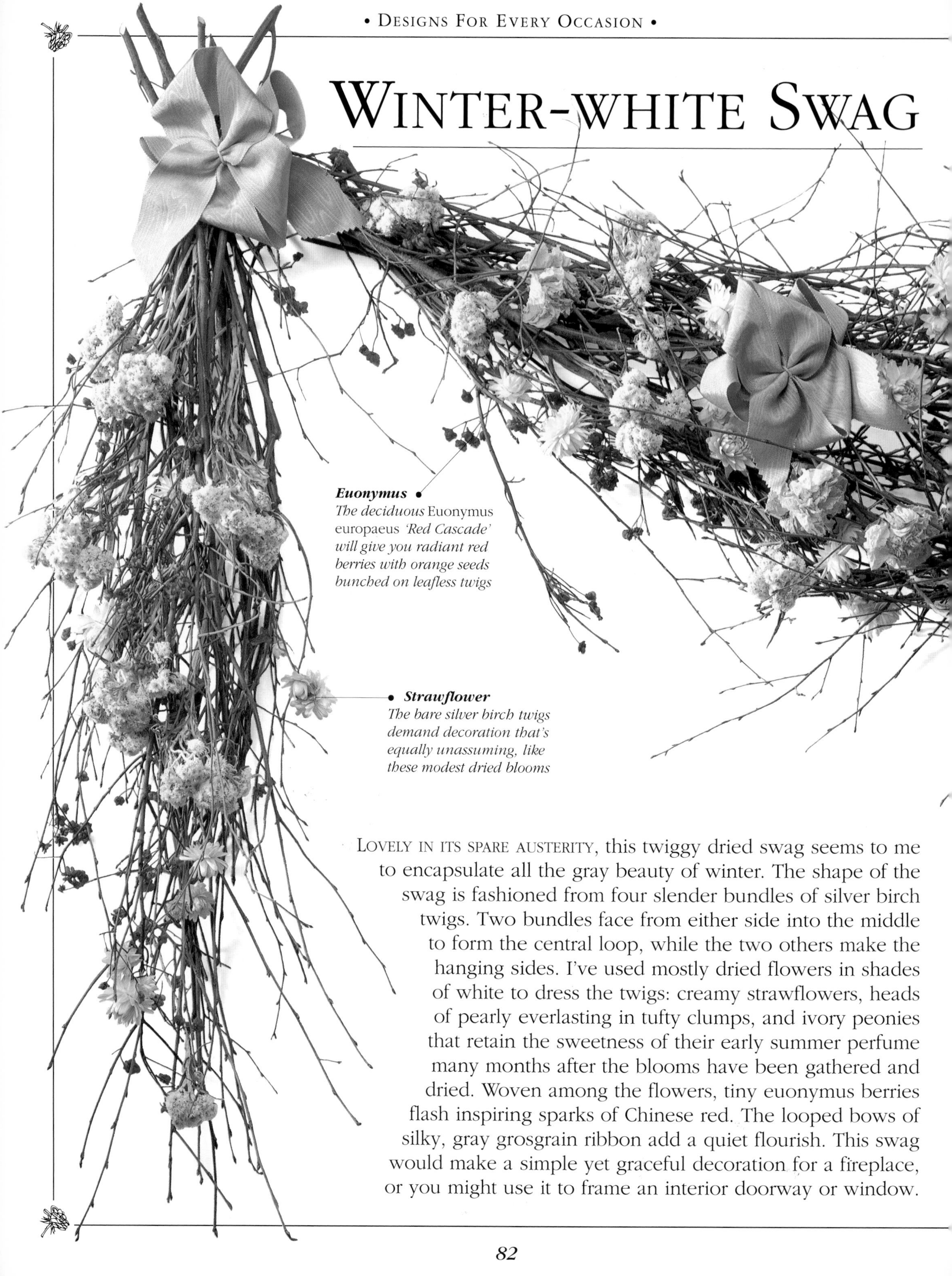

Euonymus
The deciduous Euonymus
europaeus *'Red Cascade'
will give you radiant red
berries with orange seeds
bunched on leafless twigs*

Strawflower
*The bare silver birch twigs
demand decoration that's
equally unassuming, like
these modest dried blooms*

LOVELY IN ITS SPARE AUSTERITY, this twiggy dried swag seems to me to encapsulate all the gray beauty of winter. The shape of the swag is fashioned from four slender bundles of silver birch twigs. Two bundles face from either side into the middle to form the central loop, while the two others make the hanging sides. I've used mostly dried flowers in shades of white to dress the twigs: creamy strawflowers, heads of pearly everlasting in tufty clumps, and ivory peonies that retain the sweetness of their early summer perfume many months after the blooms have been gathered and dried. Woven among the flowers, tiny euonymus berries flash inspiring sparks of Chinese red. The looped bows of silky, gray grosgrain ribbon add a quiet flourish. This swag would make a simple yet graceful decoration for a fireplace, or you might use it to frame an interior doorway or window.

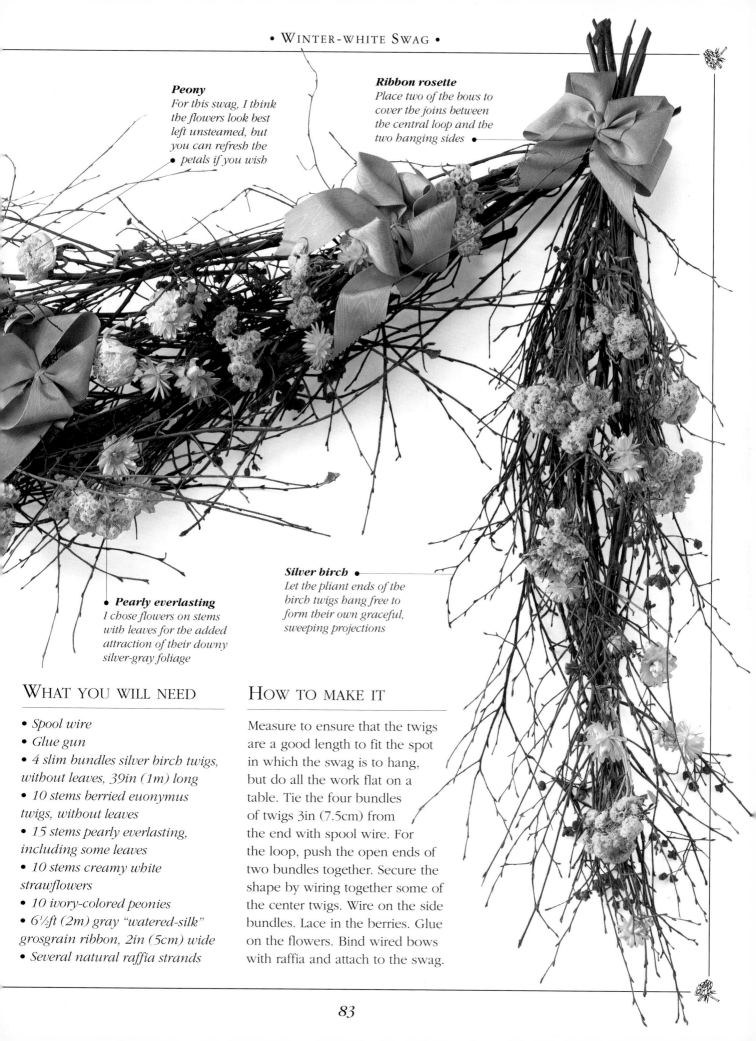

Peony
For this swag, I think the flowers look best left unsteamed, but you can refresh the petals if you wish

Ribbon rosette
Place two of the bows to cover the joins between the central loop and the two hanging sides

Pearly everlasting
I chose flowers on stems with leaves for the added attraction of their downy silver-gray foliage

Silver birch
Let the pliant ends of the birch twigs hang free to form their own graceful, sweeping projections

WHAT YOU WILL NEED

- Spool wire
- Glue gun
- 4 slim bundles silver birch twigs, without leaves, 39in (1m) long
- 10 stems berried euonymus twigs, without leaves
- 15 stems pearly everlasting, including some leaves
- 10 stems creamy white strawflowers
- 10 ivory-colored peonies
- 6½ft (2m) gray "watered-silk" grosgrain ribbon, 2in (5cm) wide
- Several natural raffia strands

HOW TO MAKE IT

Measure to ensure that the twigs are a good length to fit the spot in which the swag is to hang, but do all the work flat on a table. Tie the four bundles of twigs 3in (7.5cm) from the end with spool wire. For the loop, push the open ends of two bundles together. Secure the shape by wiring together some of the center twigs. Wire on the side bundles. Lace in the berries. Glue on the flowers. Bind wired bows with raffia and attach to the swag.

PEONY BASKET

WE'RE ACCUSTOMED to putting baskets of flowering plants outside the house, hung on garden walls, but tend to forget that they can become superb decorations for indoor rooms and halls as well. The willow basket that I've chosen for this wall hanging looks rather like a windowbox, and so I've arranged the dried flowers with their stems upright, to appear almost as if they are growing out of the basket. The arrangement is crammed with texture. Delicate campion and crisp, starry sunrays nestle between voluptuous pink peony blooms, while the shimmering, leafy oat stalks contribute quivers of pale green freshness that remind me of a wild meadow in early summer.

WHAT YOU WILL NEED

- *Woven willow basket, 15in (38cm) long, 6in (15cm) wide, & 6in (15cm) deep*
- *8 bricks dry foam*
- *Medium-gauge floral wires*
- *25 oat stalks, including some stalks with leaves attached*
- *12 stems pink peonies*
- *10 stems pink campion*
- *30 stems sunray flowers, in shades of light & darker pink*

HOW TO MAKE IT

The basket need not be protected with a plastic trash-bag lining for this arrangement because all the plant material I've used is dried. First, cut and pack bricks of dry foam into the basket so that they are firmly wedged, leaving a gap of ¾in (2cm) between the top of the foam and the upper edge of the basket. Gather the oat leaves and make up several small wired bunches of them *(see page 22)*.

Steam the peonies *(see page 17)* if their petals are squashed. Place clumps of the oat stalks into the basket first, putting some shorter clumps near the front. Add in the wired bunches of leaves. As you are building up the arrangement, remember that its overall height should be about three times the depth of the basket. Position the peonies, and add in the stems of campion and sunray flowers last.

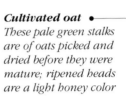

Cultivated oat •
These pale green stalks are of oats picked and dried before they were mature; ripened heads are a light honey color

Peony •
For the very best effect, place these luxuriant flowers at varying heights, from the front through to the back of the arrangement

Pink campion
Nodding catchfly is the quaint alternative name for this plant, which was once a common sight in country hedgerows •

Sunray •
Any daisylike flowers will do well here, but I chose a Helipterum species for its coy yellow flower-centers

FRUITED HOLLY FESTOON

FRUITS LOOK EXTREMELY JOLLY in garlands and swags, and especially festive when you are making a decoration for the winter holiday season. I've chosen pomegranates for this festoon, together with tamarillos and tangerines, all set among variegated holly. They are such beautiful fruits, in particular those with a deep reddy pink blush, and their availability has been extended so that you can still buy them right into midwinter. The dark red skins of the tamarillos are also stunning. Select your tangerines with care so that you get the brightest orange fruits.

WHAT YOU WILL NEED

FOR EVERY 39IN (1M) OF FESTOON
- *39in (1m) chicken wire, 12in (30cm) wide*
- *12 large handfuls damp sphagnum moss*
- *Spool wire & heavy floral wires*
- *40 sprigs variegated holly*
- *8 pomegranates, sprayed gold*
- *12 tamarillos*
- *4 firm-skinned tangerines*
- *39in (1m) metallic gold wire-edged ribbon, 1½in (4cm) wide*

HOW TO MAKE IT

This festoon is made on a RIGID BASE *(see page 26)*. Roll the chicken wire around the moss to create the base, making a wider section at the bottom of each loop. Prepare the pomegranates, and wire and stuff them with absorbent paper, as described below in the annotation. Wire the tamarillos *(see page 22)*, and the tangerines as for limes *(see page 88)*. Layer holly sprigs into the base, then wire in the fruits. Attach a ribbon bow at the apex of each loop.

• **Preparing pomegranates**
Cut out a 1in (2.5cm) hole at the base. Use a teaspoon to remove the insides. Push a bent floral wire through the top of the fruit. Stuff the shell with absorbent paper

Holly
*A much-loved feature
of the holiday season,*
Ilex aquifolium – *the
English holly – gives
us many variegated
• named cultivars*

Tangerine
*Fruits enclosed in tight,
firm skins are the best to
use, since they hold the
floral-wire fixings well
and will last longer than
• those with loose skins*

Ribbon embellishment
*Add tails and spirals of ruffled
ribbon, as well as multi-looped
bows, for an especially grand
and opulent festoon*

Frosted fruit •
*While it's still wet,
sprinkle the gold
paint with grains
of coarse sugar to
get a frosted effect*

Tamarillo
*Often called tree tomato,
this fruit not only looks
wonderful but also has
edible, juicy, succulent
flesh with a tantalizing
sweet-savory taste*

NUT AND CITRUS TREES

A CHRISTMAS TREE THAT HANGS ON A WALL always excites the most enthusiastic comment. My related pair is quite easy to put together, although they are somewhat time-consuming. Plan to start them a day or two before your festivities begin. The backing of blue spruce branches ensures that the trees will last for a couple of weeks or more, and will hold onto their needles even when the foliage has dried out. You can decorate your own tree in any way that you might dress a standing Christmas tree. I've chosen an interesting and vivacious color scheme of yellow-green fresh limes mixed with silvered walnuts and passion fruits. Both look very special set against the dusky blue-green of the spruce. Miniature white tree lights enhance the silver sparkle and give the whole creation a magically festive appearance.

WHAT YOU WILL NEED

FOR THE LARGE HANGING TREE
- *Chicken wire*
- *Fine spool wire*
- *Damp sphagnum moss*
- *Medium & heavy floral wires*
- *Glue gun*
- *One set miniature white electric tree lights*
- *8 fresh limes*
- *7 passion fruits, sprayed silver*
- *20 walnuts, sprayed silver*
- *3 large branches blue spruce*
- *Piece of bark, for the trunk*

HOW TO MAKE IT

This wall hanging is made on a MATTRESS BASE *(see pages 30–31)*. Cut sections of chicken wire to form a triangular envelope 24in (60cm) tall, 20in (50cm) across at the base, and open on one long side. Join the sections using fine spool wire, then stuff with moss to make a mattress 1in (2.5cm) thick. Join up the open side. Push a heavy floral wire through each lime, looping it back into the fruit to secure it. Push a medium wire into each passion fruit. Do the same with the nuts, securing the wires with a dot of glue. Now, starting at the base of the triangle, layer in pieces of blue spruce foliage, with the fronds facing downward. Overlap the sprays so that all the stems are covered. Make holes in the mattress from the back with a pencil. Push single lights through to the front. Attach the bark, and fruits and nuts *(see pages 30–31)*.

Small hanging tree •
You can make a tree of any size by following my instructions for the large tree: simply remember to keep the proportions the same when you scale them down or up

Fresh lime •
Deep green fruits may look prettier, but these sharp citrusy yellow ones stand out well against the foliage

Bark tree trunk •
Pieces of bark are sold at good florist's shops and garden centers

Blue spruce crown
When you're layering in
the foliage, form a circle
of shorter sprays close to
the top, then crown the
tip with a longer piece
that sticks straight up

Passion fruit
The skin is a marvelous
dark purple, so silver the
fruits on their tops only,
and sprinkle them with
a frost of coarse sugar
before the paint dries

Silvered walnuts
Spray the nuts all over
a couple of times (let
dry in between coats)
to give them a richly
lustrous finish

White tree light
My silvery scheme
looks best set off
with white lights,
but traditionalists
may want to use
colored ones

WINTER HOLIDAY WREATH

RED AND GREEN are the vibrant colors of the winter season. We see them displayed, resplendently, in the rich tones of glossy evergreen leaves and brilliant scarlet berries – colors that look forward to the renewal of growth that comes with spring. First used in England by the Romans as a festive ornament for the merrymaking of Saturnalia, berried holly is to my mind the quintessence of red and green. In this jolly holiday wreath, I've used it together with clusters of chincherinchee, pieces of blue spruce, velvety anemones, variegated foliage, larch twigs, and scarlet-plume, for a contemporary interpretation of the traditional color scheme.

WHAT YOU WILL NEED

- *14in (35cm) diameter circular wet foam wreath base*
- *Medium-gauge floral wires*
- *20 red anemones*
- *3 branches blue spruce*
- *3 stems* Euonymus fortunei *'Emerald and Gold'*
- *3 branches lichened larch twigs*
- *3 stems leafless berried holly*
- *10 stems creamy white Arabian chincherinchee*
- *5 stems scarlet-plume*
- *6½ft (2m) striped green, red, & gold silk taffeta wire-edged ribbon, 3in (7.5cm) wide*

HOW TO MAKE IT

Soak the wet foam wreath base in water until the foam has taken up enough water to be damp all the way through. Do not oversoak it, or the whole thing will drip when it is hanging up. Tie a floral wire around the top of the base. Bend the ends into a loop for hanging up the finished wreath. Wire the anemone flowers *(see page 23)*. Arrange sprigs of the blue spruce and euonymus, and short lengths of larch and holly twigs into the ring, in a single direction – here, counterclockwise. Add anemone flowers in groups, then pieces of Arabian chincherinchee, to make an informal yet balanced pattern. Place sprays of scarlet-plume last. Attach a five-looped ribbon bow at the top, with other single and double bows where you please.

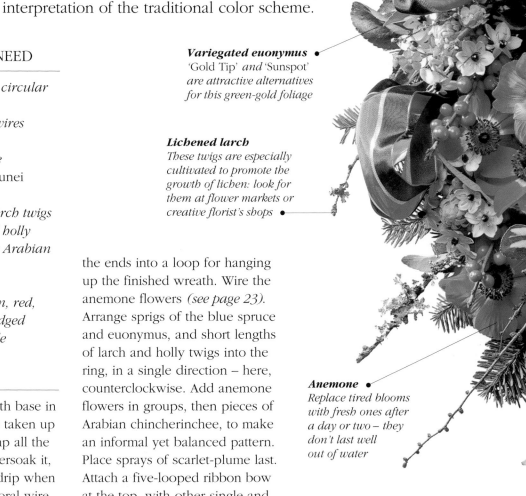

Variegated euonymus
'Gold Tip' and 'Sunspot' *are attractive alternatives for this green-gold foliage*

Lichened larch
These twigs are especially cultivated to promote the growth of lichen: look for them at flower markets or creative florist's shops

Anemone
Replace tired blooms with fresh ones after a day or two – they don't last well out of water

Blue spruce
*Luxuriant and full,
the foliage provides
a festive and gently
aromatic backdrop
for the flowers*

Scarlet-plume
*This evergreen euphorbia
carries its tiny, glowing
flowers in arching sprays
from winter into spring*

Arabian chincherinchee
*The flower centers contain
black ovaries – a stunning
contrast to the pale petals*

Berried holly
I chose winterberry (Ilex
verticillata), *a deciduous
holly that bears clusters of
bright red berries on bare
twigs all through winter*

WINTER HOLIDAY WREATH

In the midst of your other preparations for the festive season, find time to make a single spectacular decoration of fresh flowers – still something of a luxury at this time of year. Sporting gay colors to boost flagging spirits, its cheery appearance is guaranteed to banish any hint of wintry gloom. The finished wreath will last for weeks if you hang it in a cool room, or in a sheltered spot outdoors. Just pull out the anemone flowers and sprays of scarlet-plume as soon as they look past their prime, and replace them with fresh ones.

You'll find detailed instructions for making this fresh flower wreath on pages 90 and 91.

PLANT DIRECTORY

alstroemeria *Alstroemeria* Ligtu Hybrids

anemone *Anemone coronaria* De Caen Series

anthurium *Anthurium veitchii*

Arabian chincherinchee *Ornithogalum arabicum*

artemisia *Artemisia ludoviciana* var. *albula* 'Silver King', 'Silver Queen'

baby's breath *Gypsophila paniculata* 'Bristol Fairy'

bell heather *Erica cinerea*

bells of Ireland *Moluccella laevis*

bittersweet *Celastrus orbiculatus*

blue spruce *Picea pungens* f. *glauca*

borage *Borago officinalis*

bottlebrush/callistemon *Callistemon beaufortia sparsa, C. citrinus* 'Splendens'

bread wheat *Triticum aestivum*

bun moss *Grimmia pulvinata*

calendula *Calendula officinalis*

campion *Silene pendula*

carnation *Dianthus* cultivars

chrysanthemum *Chrysanthemum carinatum* 'Monarch Court Jesters'

cluster-flowered everlasting *Helichrysum italicum*

cockscomb celosia *Celosia argentea* 'Cristata'

cone wheat *Triticum turgidum*

copper beech *Fagus sylvatica* f. *purpurea*

cornflower *Centaurea cyanus*

cornus *Cornus alba* 'Elegantissima'

craspedia *Craspedia globosa*

creeping Jenny *Lysimachia nummularia* 'Aurea'

cress *Chenopodium aristatum, C. polyspermum*

cultivated oat *Avena sativa*

cypress *Chamaecyparis, Cupressus*

delphinium *Delphinium consolida* 'Blue Bee'

dogwood *Cornus alba* 'Elegantissima'

drumstick scabious *Scabiosa stellata*

English holly *Ilex aquifolium* cultivars

English ivy *Hedera helix*

English oak *Quercus robur*

euonymus *Euonymus fortunei* var. *radicans* 'Emerald and Gold'

euonymus *Euonymus fortunei* var. *radicans* 'Silver Queen'

euonymus/spindletree *Euonymus europaeus* 'Red Cascade'

euphorbia *Euphorbia fulgens*

fennel *Foeniculum vulgare*

feverfew *Chrysanthemum parthenium*

field poppy *Papaver rhoeas*

fishtail palm *Caryota mitis*

freesia *Freesia* hybrids

galax *Galax urceolata* syn. *aphylla*

gerbera *Gerbera jamesonii*

globe artichoke *Cynara cardunculus*

globe amaranth *Gomphrena globosa*

gloriosa lily *Gloriosa superba* 'Rothschildiana'

goldenrod *Solidago canadensis*

golden wattle *Acacia longifolia*

grape hyacinth *Muscari armeniacum*

Guernsey lily *Nerine bowdenii*

hebe *Hebe x franciscana* 'Variegata'

hop *Humulus lupulus*

horsetail *Equisetum hyemale*

houttuynia *Houttuynia cordata* 'Chamaeleon'

larch *Larix decidua*

larkspur *Delphinium consolida*

laurustinus *Viburnum tinus* 'Eve Price'

lavender *Lavandula spica*

lemon-scented gum *Eucalyptus citriodora*

leucadendron *Leucadendron rubrum*

lichen *Hypogymnia physodes*

lisianthus *Lisianthus russellianus*

love-in-a-mist *Nigella damascena*

mahonia *Mahonia japonica*

marigold *Tagetes erecta* cultivars

Mexican orange blossom *Choisya ternata*

miniature globe thistle *Echinops ritro*

mop-headed hydrangea *Hydrangea macrophylla*

orchid *Cymbidium, Dendrobium, Vanda*

oriental lily *Lilium* 'Pompeii'

pearly everlasting *Anaphalis yedoensis*

peony *Paeonia lactiflora*

pink pepperberry *Schinus molle*

prince's feather *Amaranathus hypochondriacus*

privet *Ligustrum vulgare*

protea *Protea* 'Blushing Bride'

protea *Protea compacta*

protea *Protea mellifera*

ranunculus *Ranunculus asiaticus*

reindeer moss *Cladonia rangiferina*

rosemary *Rosmarinus officinalis*

rose *Rosa* 'Europa', 'Golden Time', 'Landia', and other cultivars

ruscus *Ruscus aculeatus*

safflower *Carthamus tinctorius*

salvia *Salvia horminum* Art Shades Series

scarlet-plume *Euphorbia fulgens*

sheet moss *Mnium hornum*

shepherd's purse *Lunaria minima*

silver birch *Betula pendula*

silver gum eucalyptus *Eucalyptus cordata*

smilax *Asparagus asparagoides*

snow-in-summer *Euphorbia marginata*

Spanish moss *Tillandsia usneoides*

sphagnum moss *Sphagnum auriculatum* var. *auriculatum*

spindletree *Euonymus europaeus*

statice *Limonium sinuatum*

strawflower *Helichrysum bracteatum*

strelitzia/bird of paradise *Strelitzia nicolai*

sunflower *Helianthus annuus*

sunray *Helipterum roseum*

sweet marjoram *Origanum marjorana*

sweet pea *Lathyrus odoratus*

tree asparagus *Asparagus meyeri*

tuberose *Polianthes tuberosa*

tulip *Tulipa* 'Angélique'

viburnum/laurustinus *Viburnum tinus*

weeping willow *Salix x sepulcralis* 'Chrysocoma'

wild clematis/old man's beard/ traveller's joy *Clematis paniculata*

winterberry (deciduous holly) *Ilex verticillata*

yarrow *Achillea filipendulina* 'Coronation Gold'

yellow kangaroo paw *Anigozanthos flavidus*

INDEX

ACKNOWLEDGMENTS

Author's Acknowledgments

I would like to give great thanks to my partner, Quentin Roake, who has worked with me to produce this book; to Dennis, Dave, and Lee at John Austin, New Covent Garden Market, for all the magnificent flowers that they have supplied; to Machin and Henry at Creekside, South London, for their wide selection of dried plant material; to Stephen Hayward, for all his wonderful photographs, and a plentiful supply of doughnuts; and to Gillian Roberts and Debbie Myatt, who have made working on this book so pleasurable.

Publisher's Acknowledgments

Many thanks to Mark Bracey for computer support; to Deborah Myatt for the line artwork; to Mel Roberts for all his editorial help; and to Alex Corrin for the index.